POPE JOHN PAUL II ON EASTERN RELIGIONS AND YOGA

Pope John Paul II on Eastern Religions and Yoga

A Hindu-Buddhist Rejoinder

RAM SWARUP

VOICE OF INDIA
NEW DELHI

First published 1995

ISBN 81-85990-32-8

Published by Voice of India, 2/18, Ansari Road, New Delhi–110 002 and printed at Crescent Printing Works (Pvt.) Ltd., P-14, Connaught Circus, New Delhi–110 001

Contents

Preface

Pope John Paul's book *Crossing The Threshold of Hope* says nothing new; it merely reiterates Catholics' traditional position. But the book has its own importance for it carries the Pope's signature.

In this book, along with Christianity, the Pope discusses non-Christian religions — a departure from the pre-colonial era. "Other" religions have always interested the Church but there was seldom any official notice of them. They were simply considered as handiwork of the Devil, and it was the special duty of the Church to oppose them. Even at present, hundreds and thousands of missionaries are busy doing that, but this time "the other religions" have been mentioned under their own names without pejorative notice.

Pope John Paul's book discusses Judaism from which Christianity derives; it also discusses Islam, a kind of sister religion, with which Christianity had to do much from its very birth. In spite of their bitter conflicts, these religious ideologies share many things in common: a common God, common doctrines and common hatreds. The Pope mentions this fact and wants it to become the basis of a new understanding between them.

He also speaks of Buddhism and of Eastern yogic practices, and also of Europe's New Age Movement in which he sees clear Eastern influences. For our purpose, this is the most important part of the book and we have taken it the most into consideration.

Christianity is doing well outwardly so far as money, power and counting of souls is concerned, but inwardly it is facing an acute problem. The last century saw the rise of a rationalist movement which found Christianity wanting in reason. During the same period, Eastern religions have also been getting better known and their challenge has been equally far-reaching. They have shown that Christianity's spiritual and ethical worth is no better than its rational worth.

They challenge the very foundations of "revealed" religions. Christianity offers to give us a revealed truth of which it claims to be the sole custodian. The Eastern religions on the other hand tell us of a truth which is "hidden" within man himself; they say that much of man remains "unknown" to himself; they ask him to seek this "hidden" and "unknown" within himself. Thus they speak of truths which are man's own, which are part of him, which reside in every heart, and which a man seeks and finds in his deeper moments. By the same token they speak of a truth which is not mere history or historical but which is true for all time and all people. In one sense, this truth is also a revelation, manifesting what is hidden *(sannihitam)*, but it is different in conception and has little to do with revelation of revelatory religions. It is a revelation which man is ever seeking and ever finding within himself. Here there are no special messengers with their exclusive revelations and no special agencies to propagate them further. Here also are no dogmas but only verifiable truths, truths open to all. *Ehi passa*, Come and see for yourself, the Buddha says.

By the same token these truths have no geographic connotation; they are merely *Eastern* in a manner of speaking. Probably they were most developed and best preserved and still exist as a living tradition in India but they belong to all genuine seekers coming from different times and places — Egypt, Greece, Europe, the Americas, etc. Pythagoras, Plato, Apollonious, Plotinus, Stoics, Hermetists, Gnostics are fully *Eastern*. European seekers are already discovering a pre-Christian Pagan Europe which was closer to the East in its spiritual orientation. In this way they are also rediscovering their religious past and their lost Gods. It should work for their religious self-renewal.

Recently the Church has invited dialogue with other religions. For several centuries, Christianity has been at the top and it has conditioned our minds to think about it and, what is even more important, about ourselves too in a particular way. In this guided dialogue, it was expected that we would keep to these programmed thoughts. But things are now changing. Others do not think of Christianity or of themselves as it does and wants them to do. They have now their own thoughts about it as well as about themselves.

This volume could be regarded as our contribution to the above dialogue. It does not accept Christianity's view of itself and of others. It offers a different view — a Hindu-Buddhist view of both. It continues the work begun in our *The Word as Revelation: Names of Gods* and carried on in our *Hindu View of Christianity and Islam.*

The book is written in reply to the Pope's but the intention is not polemical. It could even be delinked from its immediate occasion and read independently. The idea is not to find faults but to warn against cliches, and to promote, deepen and broaden understanding of the subject and to serve truth.

RAM SWARUP

New Delhi,
12 July, 1995
Guru Purnima, 2052

1
Diehard Christianity
(Pope John Paul II on Buddhism)

Pope John Paul's new book *Crossing The Threshold of Hope* reveals a diehard Christianity. There is nothing in the 229-page book which he could not have written as Archbishop of Krakow seventeen years ago; or which is new or different from what a thousand Christian theologians have been saying for two thousand years. He merely repeats old claims. He restates the old view that Christianity is supreme among the world's religions, that the Church alone knows the truth, that there is no salvation outside it, and that even among the warring Christian sects, the Church is paramount and alone teaches the "fullness of the gospel." It will disappoint those who were expecting something different. But they are themselves to blame for entertaining such an expectation. Christianity is a prisoner of its dogmas and history.

In his book Pope John Paul discusses, among other non-Christian religions, Buddhism and Eastern Yoga also and devotes several pages to them. This kind of attention is new. Even in the Second Vatican Council which took place as late as the mid-sixties, the words Buddhism and Hinduism appeared only once in its copious documents. But it seems certain things have been happening meanwhile which have made the Church take greater notice of them. In the post-colonial era, as the two religions get better known among the Westerners, they attract the more educated, the more serious and seeking type among them. In Bangkok, for example, Pope John Paul saw the Buddhist Patriarch surrounded by Western Buddhist monks. This is bad enough and a responsible official of the Church like the Pope can no longer pretend not to notice the danger.

Pope John Paul starts by conceding that Buddhism like Christianity is a religion of "salvation". This is a great change — though a change of language and not of heart as we shall presently see. In the good old days, Eastern religions were unhesitatingly and unceremoniously declared to be religions of *damnation* from a thousand pulpits and platforms, but now the times have changed and the approach has to be more sophisticated. Hence the concession.

But the Pope feels uncomfortable in the new language, and as soon as he makes the concession he takes steps to withdraw it. He clarifies that the two salvations and their supporting doctrines "are opposed"; that the Buddhist "enlightenment" (he always puts the word within quotes suggesting that the idea is questionable) is "negative"; that it derives from the conviction that "the world is bad", and is the "source of evil and suffering". At the end, he argues that while Buddhist salvation comes from "indifference to the world", Christians free themselves "from the evil through the good that comes from God".

Excellent, though unfortunately, the Church does not prove it by its example and it does not show many instances of this good in its long history. Perhaps it thought it was enough that its God was good and he would take care of the rest. A good God has already sorted out his own and put the Church at the top. Or, perhaps the Church was good in its special way — not by human but by divine standards, according to the wishes and commandments of its God. This good included persecution and genocide of heathens and their conversion; it included Inquisition, burning of heretics in hundreds of thousands for their own good — burning their bodies in order to save their souls.

Suffering

Pope John Paul is merely repeating what Christian theologians and scholars have been saying for the last several hundred years. They have been calling Indian religions "pessimistic", "fatalistic", "other-worldly". Such views are based on unthinking cliches and they originate in ignorance about things spiritual.

Let us clarify what "suffering" means in the Indian religious thinking. It does not mean pain in the ordinary sense, nor is this pain personal. On the other hand, it is an *insight* into the nature of things. It is a realization that suffering is the necessary condition of one who follows the lower law and lower pulls of life, who pursues *anātma*, who does not *know himself* or his source, and is not aware of his transcendental dimension. But when he begins to know himself, things begin to change. He enters a new stream (*śrotāpanna*) that flows *upward*. He begins to see that his suffering is not his own; he also begins to find that the sufferings of others are also his, and he begins to develop a new compassion; he also begins to see that there is an *End* to this suffering and also a *Way* out of it. These great "noble truths" go together and "All is Suffering" does not stand alone.

The truth of Suffering has also to be read along with another great truth emphasized in the Upanishadas: that All this is Joy; that all beings are born in joy, they live in joy and they enter into joy when they cease to be their petty selves and *know* themselves.

Negation

Indian religious thought in general and Buddhism in particular are also accused of "world and life negation", as Albert Schweitzer puts it. The accusation is popular with Christian and Western writers and the Pope repeats it but it has little meaning.

The truth is that in Indian thought, *moksha* or liberation is a noble category and in certain schools finds a great emphasis. But it is always meant to enrich and raise life, not to negate it. Moreover, *moksha* has to be read along with the traditional four aims or *purusharthas* of life, or the Vedic concept of a *luminous* and heroic life lived in Gods and great truths of the Self. The physical and economic well-being is put under the guidance of *dharma* which in turn is rooted in *moksha*, or dispassion, or freedom from the pull of lower life. It is the right thing to do for no *dharma* is possible without dispassion; on the other hand, in its absence, *dharma* becomes a mere rationalization of lower life as we can see in every day life where larger truths are invoked to justify and pursue lower ends.

If we study Buddhist texts, negation there means only one

thing: negation of greed and hatred, negation of ego and delusion, negation of false views (*drishṭi)* — which would include negation of deluded ideologies and theologies, negation of infatuation with self-assumed roles like "the white-man's burden", or the "divine mandate" of the missionaries to convert the world, negation of *da'wah* and *jihād*. No doubt many would find this negation unpalatable and call it "negation of life", the only kind of life they ordinarily know having no inkling of a higher life.

Negation is eminently a Yogic concept and it is regarded as necessary for self-exceeding and self-transcendence. *Sanātana Dharma* teaches that there is much in life that has to be negated, so that life can be "affirmed" in its more luminous aspects. It teaches that there is much in you which is not *you*, which is *anātma* and, therefore, has to be rejected. On the path of Yoga, at every stage new worlds are glimpsed, but they too would not suffice a seeker who is pursuing a still higher goal. To each of these — his own self-formations — he has to learn to say: not this, not this, the *neti neti* of the Upanishads. Every denial here means a step forward, a new discovery, a new affirmation at a higher and deeper level.

And at no stage is the process joyless. Every stage has its own joys and they call for self-exceeding. Such joys cannot even be dreamt by those who talk of the "positive" approach in the usual sense of the term. The Upanishads speak of the worlds and joys of a knower of Brahma, *brahma-vid*. Similarly, admirers of the Buddha would sometimes go to him and sympathize with him for his "deprivation", but he would tell them that his life, his worlds and joys were incomparable. He would tell them about the joys of a virtuous life, the joys of *śīla* and *samādhi*, the progressively higher and joyful worlds and life of the first, second, third and fourth *dhyāna*, then further of various *ananta-samāpattis*, and lastly of the joys of *nirodha* and *nirvāṇa bhūmis*.

According to Yogic insight, the worlds and life and joys of *nirvāṇa* are not negative though they are often expressed in the language of negation; for, there is nothing to compare with them in our ordinary experience. In the same way, *nirvāṇa* is not nothingness but fullness, *pūrṇam* of the Upanishads. The world of a knower of *brahma* is clothed in celestial glory — *īśāvāsyamidam*, as the Upanishads say; but the key to it is the much-maligned renunciation, indifference and equal-mindedness (and *upekshā* and *samatā*). Non-yogic religions know nothing of these higher worlds, lives and joys.

Christian Salvation

These are the joys of which Hinduism-Buddhism speaks, the life and the worlds it discovers and affirms. But what are the joys of a Christian salvation? There is near-total silence on the subject. We are told that there is Resurrection and Judgement — and these are interpreted not as parables and morals but literally as events in the most physical terms. The man rises with his body and nothing is said about the regeneration of the soul. He rises with his old body with its same old desires, hankerings and infatuations. If he is an unbeliever, he is condemned and goes straight to hell or Fire, to a life of eternal punishment. But if he is a believer, he is "saved" and sent to heaven. Muslim theologians have spoken of the joys of the "saved" at length — untiring copulation and gormandizing. Christian theologians have added some more. One of the greatest joys of the "saved" according to them is that they would watch, from their balcony in heaven, unbelievers and heretics roasting in hell.

"Positive" Approach

While Buddhism is condemned for its negativism and pessimism, the Christian West is praised for its "positive" approach, its life-affirmation and world-affirmation. Christian scholars started this intellectual fashion and kept it alive until others also took it up. Pope John Paul continues with it and praises "Western Civilization" for its "*positive approach* to the world"; he also thanks it for its "achievements of science and technology" which, he claims, are rooted in "ancient Greek philosophical tradition and in Judaeo-Christian Revelation." This is a strange claim made by the head of an organization which waged relentless war on Greek religion, sciences and freedom; which was the author of Inquisition and which persecuted free inquiry and scientists throughout its career; which only in the last century issued its *Syllabus of Errors* (1864) which found everything wrong about science. But the Church is now trying to appropriate and claim for itself the prestige that belongs to others. So far as science is concerned, Christianity opposed it and was opposed by it for centuries. The struggle continues.

Similarly, Pope John Paul's note on "positive approach to the world" is also new. Not long ago, Christianity took pride in being "*other-worldly*". It talked of the "pilgrim Church"; it talked of "the last things". In fact, the Bible is full of them, and the apostles and early Church fathers were expecting the end of the world any day.* But now under different pressures, preoccupation with the "last things" has receded. The Church now takes pride in being *worldly* or rather *third-worldly*, a cruel form of its worldliness. In this, it is trying to give itself a new doctrinal face in order to keep in line with the current intellectual fashion or *zeitgeist*.

But whether it calls itself this-worldly or other-worldly makes no difference for both are projections of an external mind; both lack innerness and compassion. Under either name the nature and aims of the Church have remained unchanged and it has continued to play a cruel and destructive role; it has taught and exercised strong hatred

* Under this motif, the Bible taught, according to some theologians, only an "interim ethics." The "day of the lord", a name for the "end of the world", was "at hand." It could dawn any time. There was hardly any time left either for "marriage or for giving in marriage." Throughout the medieval age, even though the Church played most sordid realpolitik, it remained strongly other-worldly in its theology. Innocent III, before he became Pope, wrote on the "Wretchedness of Man's Condition". He taught: "How filthy the father, how low the mother, how repulsive the sister." He wrote: "We who shrink from touching, even with the tips of our fingers, a gob of phlegm or a lump of dung, how is it that we crave for the embraces of this mere bag of night-soil?"— his name for woman. (Rejection of woman did not prevent him though from playing power-politics to the hilt. He excommunicated kings of France and England, laid their countries under an interdict, and obliged them to submit; he presided over the Fourth Crusade and the Albigensian Crusade.) Throughout its career,

and enmity towards "unbelievers"; it has been making pretentious claims and has been assuming an egoistic and deluded role. Its whole approach is based on spiritual arrogance and deluded assumptions — on *anātma*, to put it in Buddhist language. The same applies to Islam too, its sister religion.

Buddhist protest

Sri Lankan Buddhists were angry and protested against the Pope's view of Buddhism. They refused to receive him during his recent visit to their country; the Sri Lankan Government employed, quite unnecessarily though, thirty thousand strong squad of police and selected armed forces to "protect" the unwanted guest.

In this episode, while the Buddhist protest is new, Christianity's view of Buddhism is old. The Pope himself has said nothing new and has merely repeated the old Church position. If the Sri Lankan

the Church taught that sin and sex are synonymous and it has been part of its theology. The Bible had taught that people should become "eunuchs for the kingdom of heaven's sake." This teaching remained a strong streak in Christianity until recent times. John Wesley, founder of Methodists (1729A.D.), four days after deciding to marry, advised his single followers to remain single for the kingdom of heaven's sake "except when a particular case might be an exception to the general rule" (quoted in *Enthusiasm* by R.A.Knox). But now things are changing and exceptions are becoming the general rule. In the new Freudian world, Pope John Paul finds sex "beautiful". The Anglican Church has gone further. It is adjusting its moral teachings to "changing circumstances" — to the current moral practices of its members. It finds its members increasingly living outside marriage in a state which the Bible describes as "living in fornication and sin." The Anglican bishops now recommend that the Church ceases to be "judgmental" and the biblical phrase be abandoned altogether. The Church also finds couples, gay and lesbian, freely cohabiting together; its bishops find no fault in it and say that "love of God is lived out in a variety of ways", and that "homosexual partners create high quality." Altogether the Anglican bishops have now a *broader* and non-biblical view of the family and they "support families in all their diversity." They find that in their new ways of coming together (their equally frequent parting is not mentioned here) and cohabitation, the new couples are "expressing their deepest commitments." Rev. Richard Holloway, Bishop of Edinburg, says that adultery is not a sin, for man was born for love and humans were meant to have many lovers and not be faithful to their mates.

Buddhists were expecting a different view of Buddhism from him they were mistaken. As the Supreme Pontiff of the Church, he must express its views which it has never hidden. It has a "divine mandate" and it must convert. Earlier, the Pope had told the Christian clergy at the Asian Bishops' Conference at Manila: "A great harvest of faith will be reaped in this vast and vital continent." In Sri Lanka, he also beatified one Joseph Vaz, an 18th century missionary, whom he described as a man "on fire with faith". The Church beatification or canonization is often a political act and it speaks for itself. It shows what kind of men the Church still honours. Adding insult to injury, the Pope made his views very clear: the heathen country needs the continued attention of the Church.

This view is not only of the Catholics alone but is shared by many other denominations of Christianity. For example, the Texas-based *Gospel of Asia* introduces Sri Lanka as "a country forgotten by many... but has received much attention from the devil." India shares this honour with Sri Lanka in the eyes of the devil. The same paper says that "the enemy (Satan) has used Hinduism to enslave India in a system that dooms her people to misery in this world, as well as to an eternity in hell." Pat Robertson, an evangelist, candidate for US Presidency in 1988 election, shows no greeter charity or larger mental horizon. In a TV talk of the 700 Club (March 23, 1995), he described Hinduism as "demonic" and India as "a nation in bondage to spiritual forces that have deceived many for thousands of years." Earlier he had come to India on a missionary jaunt to help Hindus to "confess their faith in Christ and receive a touch from heaven, and be set free from a lifetime of fear and demonic oppression." The Pope is saying the same thing in more polite language. We should be thankful to him.

Weeds grew while Eastern religions like Taoism, Buddhism and Hinduism slept. They should wake up now and work for self-renewal and, in the process, also work for the renewal of man's spiritual heritage which has been under the attack of fanatic semi-religious ideologies.

2
Yogic and non-Yogic Religions
(Pope John Paul on Eastern Yogic Practices)

Many Christians failing to find deeper and inner satisfaction in their ideology are taking to Yoga, and the Church is very much concerned. In December 1989, the Vatican's Sacred Congregation for the Doctrine of the Faith, the Pope's guardian of orthodoxy, issued a 23-page document approved by the present Pope himself. It was addressed to its Bishops. It sounded a warning against Yoga techniques. It said that "one can take from them what is useful so long as the Christian conception of prayer, its logic and requirements are never obscured." The *Atlanta Journal and Constitution* of December 15, 1989 reporting the news also commented that it was "the first time the Vatican addressed publicly the problems raised by the strong attraction for some Catholics of methods inspired by Eastern religions such as Hinduism and Buddhism."

The Pope repeated this warning quoting from this document. He says: "It is not inappropriate *to caution* those Christians who enthusiastically welcome *certain ideas originating in the religious traditions of the Far East* — for example, techniques and methods of meditation... In some quarters these have become fashionable... First one should know one's own spiritual heritage well and consider whether it is right to set it aside lightly." He has to sound a warning against this tendency towards interiority for it could be the undoing of the Church.

Biblical Tradition

Yoga of Eastern tradition has no place in traditional Christianity. The Bible shows no trace of it. The leading ideas of the

New Testament are very different. They are sin, repentance, the expected end of the world. This inspired certain spiritual practices in Christianity which were active throughout the most part of its career. During the medieval period, Franciscan Salimbene tells us, "All men, both small and great, noble knights and men of the people, scourged themselves naked in procession through the cities, with the bishops and men of religion at their head... if any would not scourge himself he was held worse than the Devil." In a milder form this practice prevails even today. Meetings called 'Revivals' are organized where crowds of pious Christians weep loudly over their sins. It gives them a strange kind of exaltation; they feel light after that and probably also renewed for more sins.

In the New Testament, we also meet another practice called "prophesying" or "speaking in strange tongues." People foregathered in a congregation and waited for the Holy Ghost to speak through them. The result was a big confusion. People gibbered; they spoke all at one time. St. Paul found it all "mad." He said that what they said should be intelligible to all others present and also "impress the strangers that may be in their midst" (1 Cor 14.24).

This practice had its difficulties which had to be sorted out. In what people spoke, it was not sure what came from the Holy Ghost and what came from the Devil who was active from the start to thwart the work of the Church. St. Paul gave a simple solution. He said that what accorded with the gospel was from God and the rest from the Devil. "No one who is led by God's Spirit can say 'A curse on Jesus!' and no one can confess 'Jesus is the Lord', unless he is guided by the Holy Spirit," he said. The Holy Ghost must confirm holy Catholic theology.

This problem was to continue to dog the Church all along. Even today, the directors of souls are busy sorting out what is from God and what is from the Devil. Pious Christians in all ages have been visited by the apparitions of Jesus and Mary and

Christian saints and receiving all kinds of visions, voices and revelations. The phenomena are not rare and they are taking place all the time. The senior theologians have often provided rough and ready rules for the guidance of the directors of souls. For example, Jesus would not appear nude, or deformed in limbs, or take an animal form. If so, those apparitions are from the Devil. There are also certain things which the Devil would not do. For example, he will not take the form of a dove or a lamb because these are symbols of the Holy Ghost and of Christ.

Similarly, revelations of a woman are false if it tells her to direct and counsel the clergy or the princes for "this is not the part that women shall play in the Church." In the same way, revelations which expose the vices of the clergy and the Church and cause *scandal* are from the Devil. The problem is vast and we can merely touch it here to point to its nature.

But the promptings of the Devil were often less innocent than would appear from the above. He was busy everywhere but particularly in monasteries and nunneries (read Aldous Huxley's *Devils of Loudon*) and in the Christian countryside. Here men and women made pacts with the Devil; women even copulated with him though without much satisfaction for his organs were icy cold. He in return gave them power to fly by night, make their neighbours impotent and cast spell on their cattle. Women were his worst victims. We are informed by a Newsletter of the day that "more than 300 wretched women in the county of Gulch consorted with the Devil... eighty-five of them were punished in the fire on the 6th May, 1591." The Newsletter added that it was being "committed to print so that it may serve as a warning to all honest women and maids."

In many cases, it was difficult to find out where the Devil ended and God began. For example, Thomas Schucker, a Swiss Anabaptist, was divinely ordered to cut off his brother's head and he did it in the presence of their parents. Probably his scale was unimpressive and therefore he is likely to be judged less kindly by us now; but those who were divinely inspired to cut off the heads of hundreds of thousands of pagans, infidels and heretics are on the honoured roster of saints and prophets. The Christian sinners are often better than Christian saints.

Borrowings

Christianity is not all Biblical. From an early period, it heavily leaned on many non-Biblical traditions. For example, the Bible gives no support to an ascetic ideal. In fact, Jesus himself had a reputation, unlike John the Baptist, of being "gluttonous and a wine bibber" (Mat 11.19). But as Christianity progressed, we find in it a rich monastic life from an early stage. It had its source in a pre-Christian era. From very early days, we find hermits all over Egypt and Palestine; they lived in community and also alone; they lived in deserts or deserted places and on mountain tops. They were often Buddhist in their ethics and the monastic forms in which they lived probably also derived from the same source. As competing religions were made to withdraw, we find these communities becoming an important limb of Christianity.

Similarly, the Bible gives little evidence of a contemplative life. All that we find there in the way of a religious life is prayer and preaching, the miracles of Jesus, and claims made for him as a saviour. But at a much later stage some elements of contemplative life were also added to Christianity though they always remained weak and were often resisted.

In the earliest phase, Christianity borrowed from the neo-Platonists and the Gnostics, whose thought had great kinship with Vedanta as we shall see. But later on, when this source dried up, its monks began to borrow directly from the Eastern sources. They borrowed not only the rosary, but also deeper things that touch on spiritual practices and techniques and ideas; they borrowed certain breathing exercises and Yogic practices like *prāṇāyāma* and *japam*. Monks of the Greek Orthodox

Church instructed their followers "to join to every breath a sober invocation of Jesus." They borrowed certain *deśa-bandhas*, the knowledge of psychic centres in the body. The *Hesychasts* (the quiet or calm ones) in the Greek Orthodox Church were accused of teaching people "to breathe in divine grace through the nostrils"; they talked of "leading the mind inside the body and hold it there"; they were called *navel-gazers*, and nicknamed *omphalo-psyches*, or people whose soul was in their navel. In Carthusian monasteries, they learned to contemplate on "death", the great *maraṇānusmriti* of Indian Yoga. Trappists took it up in later centuries.

In Latin Christendom, however, Eastern ideas and practices of meditation came through another channel. A Syrian monk, disciple of the celebrated Proclus (b. A.D. 412; head of the Neo-Platonist school at Athens, a mystic and writer — among his many writings is also his *Eighteen Arguments against the Christians*), wrote several treatises including *De mystica theologia* under the ghost-name of Dionysius, a Greek whom St. Paul had converted. Under this mistaken identity, his writings got a footing in Christianity. After several centuries, they were translated by Scotus Erigena.[1] And these translations became the basis of Rhineland mystics of whom the tallest was Eckhart. Fortunately he died before he caught the attention of the Inquisition. Twenty-eight articles from his sermons and writings were condemned after his death by Pope John XXII in 1329.

It is this borrowed tradition which is often described as "Christian mysticism." And it is to this that those who love to see a perennial tradition in all religions refer. But it remained

1. Scotus Erigena was himself an oustanding thinker of his age. His conception of God was not of Christian theology. His God was in all things; he could only be expressed in the language of negation. To him, heaven, hell and the Garden of Eden were not physical places. He believed that all things were immortal including animals. The Pope wrote to King Charles the Bald who had given him protection that he "may no longer give poison to those who seek for bread." Erigena had to withdraw from the Court and go to a monastery in England where, it is said, he was "pierced with the iron-pens of the boys" and died.

uninfluential. The Church remained indifferent to it. Abbot J. Chapman informs us that Thomas Aquinas, the great Church theologian who wrote on every conceivable subject, says little on the subject of "mystical theology." Dominicans following the example of their leader ignored it and the Jesuits denied it altogether. At times, the works of Tauler and Suso were forbidden altogether in Jesuit circles. They had their own *Spiritual Exercises* which were more in consonance with their own temper as well as Christian theology. In short, this tradition remained restricted and hardly entered the Christian mainstream. Practical-minded churchmen thought that contemplation gave more trouble than it was worth; others like Bousset saw the danger of the dogmatic truth being obliterrated by "a cabal of mystics, dominated by women."

Yoga comes into fashion

But now that the West has opened to the East, Yoga and mysticism are getting known, and it is no longer practical or prudent to ignore it. The words "experience" and "states of consciousness" hardly ever heard before in Christian circles are now routinely on the lips of missionaries and Christian theologians. Even the televengelists are talking incessantly of "experience" and "states of consciousness."

The Protestants as a whole do not understand the phenomenon of Yoga much but the more ardent of them are dealing with it in their own practical way. Some enterprising groups invent or hire Indian "yogis" to reach and propagate Baptist conclusions. One of such "yogis is Rabi" R. Maharaj. His account has been published under many titles : *Escape into the Light*, *Rebirth of a Yogi*, and now *Death of a Guru*. The account is complete with cow, snake, yogi — the usual stereotypes about India which were once popular in the West and still are among the uneducated. From this account, we learn that the gentleman was a Hindu, a brahmin, a guru, a yogi. The hero says that he began as a cow-worshipper;

that he "at the age of five practised Yoga and meditation consciously"; that once he was attacked by a snake, whether real or imagined is not clear; that for protection he called on Siva, Krishna, Vishnu and the whole host of Hindu pantheon but to no avail; and that then he called on Jesus, and lo! the snake "bolted like lightning." This book was sponsored by *Spiritual Counterfeit Projects*, California. It is introduced as the personal account of a man who struggled "to choose between Hinduism and Christ", and published "at a time when Eastern mysticism, religion and philosophy fascinate many in the West."

Catholics, particularly those involved in "dialogue" with Hinduism, tend to tackle the problem with more sophistication. They now speak of Christian experience instead of Christian theology. Many of them have started "ashrams" in India; they tell us of a *unique* Christian mysticism; they make a distinction between a Hindu Yogi and a Christian saint and their different approaches: while the one pursues supreme identity, the other pursues supreme communion; while the one is merged or rather submerged in the Impersonal Absolute, the other is utterly confronted with the Absolute in Person; while the one is pure Self without any Thou, the other is open to the divine Thou from the very depth of his Self; while the one lives in *advaita* without a second, the other lives face to face with God in interpersonal communion; while the one cultivates interiority in vertical experiences, the other seeks exteriority in horizontal acts of charity and social action; and so on. They talk of Impersonal Brahma of the Hindus and the Personal God of the Christians with pretty familiarity as if these entities are in their day's work. The monks connected with Saccidananda Ashram,[2] Dist. Tiruchirapalli, started

2. The Ashram was started in post-colonial period by two French Catholic Fathers, Jules Monchanin and Henri le Saux, both no more; their work was continued by the late Bede Griffiths. They all assumed the names and dress of Hindu sannyasins. We have discussed the problem more fully in our essay on "Liberal" Christianity included in our *Hinduism vis-a-vis Christianity and Islam*. For further discussion, see Sita Ram Goel's *Catholic Ashrams*

this pompous fashion. In all this, one can see much spiritual name-dropping, and an attempt to give themselves a position and role where they had none. One hardly heard of these things fifty years ago, and it is a very recent self-discovery on their part. But while saying all this, the missionary agenda is not forgotten. They keep telling us of an *Unknown Christ of Hinduism*, or of a *Christ in India*, or of a *Christ as Common Ground between Christianity and Hinduism*.

The Church now speaks of a *Christian* mysticism which is superior to anything known in the East. It may have some similarities with Eastern practices, we are told, but it is unique and unsurpassed in conception. Cardinal Joseph Ratzinger, president of the Sacred Congregation for the Doctrines of the Faith (a new name given since 1965 to the old, notorious Holy Inquisition), sending out warning against Eastern systems of meditation says that unlike them the "Christian meditation is not submersion in an impersonal divine atmosphere, in any abyss without face or form."

In his book, Pope John Paul repeats all this. Comparing Eastern and Catholic mysticisms he says that "despite similar aspects" there is "a fundamental difference" between the two. Categories of negative/positive which we have already met are freely used. We are told that the Buddhist *nirvāṇa* is a state of "indifference with regard to the world." Making further clarification, the Pope says that unlike Buddhist mysticism, Christian mysticism is "not born of a purely negative enlightenment"; on the other hand, it is "born of the *Revelation of the Living God*." A living God in the Biblical tradition is one who had a covenant first with the Jews and then later throwing them overboard with those who believed in his Son. The Christian history gives us some living idea of how living and kicking this God has been — a veritable militant and even terrorist of the Church's cause.

Answering those who see in Christian mysticism an Eastern inspiration, and also to establish its superiority, the Pope specially mentions John of the Cross. He says that his "mysticism begins at the point where the reflections of Buddha end." However, not many who know the subject better would agree with him. For example, Abbot John Chapman, a Benedictine and a spiritual director who wrote in the beginning of this century, said that John's mysticism was hardly Christian, that in fact John was a secret Buddhist. He said that John was like "a sponge full of Christianity: you can squeeze it all out and the full mystical theory remains. Consequently, for fifteen years or so I hated St. John of the Cross and called him a Buddhist... Then I found that I had wasted fifteen years so far as prayer was concerned."

But the Pope is right in his own way. Whatever source might have influenced John in his contemplative practices, he remained a Catholic in his loyalty and he could not break the four walls of its theology, nor did he ever seek to do it. For example, he never thought of squeezing out Jesus or Jesusism though he was ready to squeeze out God. He says: "With the coming of Christ, God has as it were become dumb and has no more to say, since that which He spoke aforetime to the prophets, He has now spoken altogether in Him, giving us all which is His Son."[3]

Śīla, Samādhi, Prajñā

But what did Christianity exactly borrow from Eastern religions and what did it make of those borrowings? In the Yogic tradition of *Sanātana Dharma*, three things are mentioned together: *śīla* (ethical life; also called *yama* and *niyama*), *samādhi* (more systematic meditative and contemplative practices), and

3. It seems that Christian mysticism failed to change the personality of its practitioners. John of the Cross, for example, even after he had written his mystical works, continued with his self-scourgings, a popular practice among Christian ascetics. Many Christian saints including Francis of Assisi remained stout missionaries. Similarly, Teresa, a mystic and a senior colleague of John, favoured missionary work among the heretics and the pagans. Soon after they died, their order of Reformed Carmelites sent a mission to Persia, and later on to unfortunate America. We are told that among them "were several martyrs"—an ominous thing. It is clear that the Christian "mystics" remained weak in spiritual *prajñā*, which is so highly valued in Hindu-Buddhist Yogas.

prajñā (spiritual wisdom). They are related but they are not the same. There are all kinds of *samādhis*, but those based on *śīla* alone are welcome. Similarly, there are *samādhis* which lead to quietude and tranquility; they are useful but they do not always lead to *prajñā*, or insight, or enlightenment.

Christianity borrowed certain spiritual practices relating to *samādhi* or, in the Christian context, *prayer*; Christianity as a rule only knew preliminary, *active* forms of prayer: — verbal, discursive and affective. The Eastern influence through various channels, some of them mentioned above, deepened its concept and practice of prayer. It gave Christian monks *passive* forms of prayer — like the prayers of *quiet* and *union* and taught them not to distrust them. But the influence could go no farther. The great *truth of upekshā* or *samatā* of the Indian Yogas hardly plays any part though "holy indifference" is mentioned here and there, particularly by the unknown author of *The Cloud of Unknowing*. *Samatā* opens higher terrains of which Christian mysticism even in its borrowed plumes shows no trace.

Thus the Indian influence though important for many reasons could not go far enough. It gave Christian monks greater warmth but not light; it deepened their emotions but could not open up their mind; it gave them ecstasy but not *prajñā*, insight into the nature of things; it gave them quiet or *śamatha* (though it remained suspect in the eyes of the Church), but not *samyak drishṭi*; it gave them a deepened at-one-ment or union with their worshipped deity but not enlightenment or awakening — *Sambodhi*. *Advaita*, liberation, and the great Vedic truths like "Reality is One, the wise call him by many names" — and the larger spiritual formulations of Indian spirituality like All is Joy or All is Suffering eluded them. They also did not realize man's status as a *purusha*, a *person*, a consciousness; he remained a *creature* though a special creature with a right to lord over other creatures.

Indian Yogic influence was unsafe for Christianity's theology and if allowed to go further threatened to topple it altogether. Therefore it was resisted and Christianity remained stuck to its own *prajñā*, or ideology — a God who denied *other* Gods, an *ummah* or church which denied other churches, a God who made himself known to the believers only through a mediator, sinfulness of man, vicarious atonement, a special saviour, superiority of the Church, hell for the unbelievers to whom no virtue would avail, etc.

Kleśas

An important aim of Indian higher Yoga is the conquest of *kleśas*,[4] or the forces that keep a man bound to lower impulsions and perspective, to a life of love and hate (*kāma-krodha*), ego and delusion — we will not describe the *kleśas* further here. The

4. Christianity has no such concept or even its near equivalent. True, we find Christian monks grappling with "sin" and temptations of Satan. These temptations often relate to concupiscence (roughly *kāma* of the Hindu Yoga) but seldom to anger (or *krodha*, the other term in the Hindu pair of *kāma-krodha*), specially anger directed against "pagans". Then it becomes "righteous anger" and is normal to a Christian. We may cite the example of St. Benedict. Jilted in love, he left the city and went out to live in a deserted place. But however hard he tried to forget his lady, her memory would not leave him. In desperation, he jumped into a nearby thorny bush, and he came out of it "wounded in body but cured in soul." Then he lived for some years a life of such self-denial that he acquired great fame and was much in demand. He decided to set up a chapel. This he did by demolishing a Pagan temple dedicated to Apollo on Monte Cassino; he "shattered the idol, cast down the altar, and burned down the sacred grove in which the people had 'sweated in their sacrilegious sacrifices' from time immemoral" (G.G. Coulton, *Five Centuries of Religion*, Vol. I) and converted it into his monastery (529 A.D., the year which also saw the forcible closure of the Athenian school of philosophy); this monastery in time became the most famous in Latin christendom. There is no account that Benedict had any problem with his *dvesha*, his hatred for the pagans, and felt called upon to overcome it in any way. This is true of almost all Christian "saints", whether before or after Benedict. Nine hundred years after him, St. Xavier, Apostle of the East, is doing the same in India. He tells us how he "ordered that everywhere the temples of the false gods be pulled down and idols broken", and when it was done, he "knows not how to describe the joy" he feels at this spectacle.

Yogic teachers say that *kleśas* have deep roots, that they come up again and again, that they take on many disguises and express themselves in many ways. They live in our best actions and thoughts — in our fasts, vigils, charities, martyrdom, prayers and theologies. From mere passions of the moment, they become ideas and ideals, doctrines, commandments, categorical imperatives. Thus idealized and *ideolized*, they become permanent hatred and permanent infatuations.

Yogic teachers further tell us that these *kleśas* are temporarily quieted down in *samādhi*; that in that state they go underground losing nothing of their shaping power; that there they live as seed-powers ready to reappear at their own time, in their own ways and by their own laws. They further tell us that only in *prajñā* they are fully conquered and lose their power of self-formation.

Christianity, however, had no such concept and it sought no such *prajñā*; it exulted in its own vision which remained infected with *kleśas*. Thus the work of deeper self-purification could not even begin and Christian theology remained *deluded* and its gods *tainted* — angry, partisan and psychically limited and poor; no wonder, it also remained burdened with an *illusory* missionary role.

The Indian Yogic system stresses the importance of a *right* "object" of meditation (*karma-sthāna*); it should be pure. Opened to higher influences, it is further purified, raised and amplified; unknown inner doors open; new Gods are born; man's higher nature is revealed. But if the *karma-sthāna* is impure and if it is under the influence of a deluded ideology or narrow dogma, the results are negative. The dogmas of jealous gods and exclusive prophets and chosen people only feed hegemonic impulses and produce religions of persecution, *jihād* and missions.

Yoga says that *śīla* is purified by *samyak-samādhi* (right *samādhi*) and *samyak-samādhi* by *samyak-prajñā* (right insight). But the reverse is equally true and happens often enough. A deluded *prajñā* defiles *samādhi* which further makes a man's *śīla* worse. One can easily see that the Christian ideology is not calculated to purify Christian *samādhi* and *śīla*. No wonder that Christian men of God have often been worse than ordinary Christians. The Christian saints have been as a rule great ideologues and practitioners of persecution.

Revelatory religions have no worthwhile theory of self-purification, particularly purification of the more hidden parts of the mind. All that they have in that line is the theory of *inspiration*, or the doctrine of the holy ghost or spirit — a veritable psychological trap. One part of the mind waits upon another part, both equally impure; one part listens, the other speaks, and the message of the one is often no better than the understanding of the other. All the *kleśas* crowd in and become voices, visions and revelations from above.

Revelatory religions have several features but they are best described as religions of *dvesha* — hatred and denial *(nirākaraṇa)* of others. *Dvesha* is a great psychic force but by itself and on its own it could not acquire the governing place, prestige, passion, permanence, focus and unnatural importance it has in these religions. It has powerful allies and it goes along with its companion-idea, *rāga*, self-love; the two in turn are held together by *aham*, by a systematic self over-valuation; and the roots are fed by a deluded theology, by the darkened counsel of a poisoned ideology, a false view *(mithyādrishṭi)* of Gods and men.

Yoga Superfluous in Christianity

The important question, therefore, is not whether Christianity borrowed from the Eastern Yogic practices but whether it could derive much benefit from them. Put in this way, the question acquires a different orientation, and it becomes clear that by the very nature of its ideational system, higher Yoga could neither be borrowed by it nor be useful to it.

Yogas cannot be borrowed or lent so easily though our new

wise men who visit the West advise differently. They go about saying that Yoga is compatible with any theology and ideational system. It is only true about preliminary physical and mental practices but not higher Yoga. Higher Yoga in *Sanātana Dharma* is organic to it. It derives from its basic intuition that there is a vast life hidden in man's inner being — Gods, worlds and realities; that here is also the source of his true life. In the normal course, a man is not aware of them and they cannot be known by a sense-bound mind. But they are known in a purified state of consciousness, by a mind deepened, raised, uplifted and illumined. Yoga is a name for raising the mind, for undertaking an inner journey. On this journey, man's provisions are *śraddhā*, *vīrya*, *smriti*, *dhyāna*, *dhāraṇā*, *samādhi*, self-reflection, surrender. The Gita mentions several other connected qualities, *daiva-sampad.*

But Christianity believes differently. It says that man is a sinner and he is saved (*redeemed* and *justified* are two other words used in this context) by the death or blood of Jesus. Man sinned *vicariously* through Adam, the first man, and was also saved *vicariously* by Jesus, the last Adam, who offered his life to propitiate a wrathful God. The whole thing is taken literally and historically and any attempt to explain it figuratively or as a parable or moral is stoutly resisted.

It is obvious that such a doctrine needs no Yoga; there is nothing hidden, nothing more to know either about God, or about oneself. All is already known. The only thing is to believe. God forgives believing sinners. "He that believes in him is not condemned; but he that believeth not is condemned already" (Jn 3.18)

It is also obvious that such a doctrine needs none of those qualities of the soul which Yoga values and which it feels are necessary for raising the level of consciousness; it does not need the *daiva-sampad* of the Gita, therefore it does not cultivate them. What for? There is a readymade God, and a readymade saviour, a ready-made deputy of him on the earth, and a Church to take care of all your spiritual concerns. You believe and obey and the rest is automatic.

Thus Christianity, doctrinally speaking, has no elements of mysticism though it is another matter that in practice it could not do without them altogether. Man is a worshipper and he must worship. He may not have a developed system of Yoga, but he must believe and worship. Belief and faith are important truths of the spirit. But let us not become their merchants.

Mysticism and Revelatory Religions

Mysticism and revelatory religions differ in other ways too. In revelatory religions, God reveals himself or his will to a privileged intermediary who in turn conveys it to his people. In mysticism, an individual has to find the truth for himself. He does it partly by becoming that truth. The truth raises him and thus raised he is also enabled to receive the truth. But in revelatory ideologies, truth is revealed to a favoured medium; it comes to him unprepared and it leaves him unchanged;[5] it comes to him unannounced and leaves him without a trace; it leaves him as it found him; and it makes no difference for was he not merely a conveyer, a messenger?

In this kind of revelation, when once God has thus revealed

---

5. Within the framework of their primary single revelation, the revelatory religions do allow subordinate revelations which strengthen the main one. They occur under all conditions and require no special preparation. Luther had his revelation while sitting on the privy in the lavatory. It told him that he was sinful but it was alright (and even commendable, for the more one sins, the more it gives Jesus chance to save—"Be a sinner, and sin boldly, but believe more boldly still," Luther said) and that his faith in Jesus as a saviour alone was enough to "justify" him. The revelation made him a reformer but it did nothing to reform him — it did not improve his tongue or heart; it gave him strength to oppose indulgences, but no new religious vision, and he remained within the traditional theological circle of sin-saviour syndrome; it hardened him against the Pope, but it did not soften him against the Jews, the women, the heretics and the poor peasants. The quantum of compassion at his disposal did not increase.

himself, he is to be received by others. It is often done by propaganda and sword. Iqbal, the modern Muslim theologian, says this much to his God: Who cared for you or called upon your name; it was the sword of Islam that did it.

Spiritual Exercises

Indian Yoga is not congenial to the Christian ideational system, but Christianity developed a form suited to its religious ideology. This we find in the form of Ignatius Loyola's *Spiritual Exercises*. Here meditation is used not for spiritual liberation as in Hinduism and Buddhism but for the intensification of certain emotions and roles. It is used to turn out Christ's soldiers and even his incendiaries.[6]

Non-Yogic Religions

Religion is not one uniform thing. Religions come from different depths of our being and have different levels of purity. There are Yogic religions and there are non-Yogic religions, and they project their own Gods and ethics. A narrow and impure source gives us narrow and impure Gods — egoistic Gods, hegemonic Gods; it even gives us a God of booty (*infāl*) who promises to give his followers cities they did not build, and wells that they did not dig, and vineyards and orchards they did not plant. Such a God is hardly a spiritual being but he is very attractive to certain religious ideologies. We have discussed the problem in our *Hindu View of Christianity and Islam* and need not dilate upon it here.

---

6. Here the exercistants also dwell on what they call Jesus's Passion. Higher spirituality and Yoga discourage fantasy but these exercises cultivate it to the point of hallucination. Their practitioners seek and sometimes receive not purification but certain physical manifestations called stigmata. Dr. Imbert who studied the subject found that this phenomenon began with St. Francis of Assisi in the thirteenth century, and after that he reckoned 321 cases of stigmatics, sixty-two of them canonized saints or Beati.

Revelatory religions provide an inhospitable soil for any developed mysticism. Anwar Shaikh, author of *Eternity* and editor of *Liberty*, says that it forms no natural part of them and it is "contrary to their fundamental principles." They are religions of *inspiration*, not of illumined reason, or illumined *buddhi* and quickened *dhī* of the famous *Gāyatrī mantra* of the Hindus. Once Apollonius, the great saint of the Graeco-Roman world, while discussing philosophy with a king told him to "avoid the kind that claims to be inspired: people like that lie about gods, and urge them to do many foolish things."

3

He that is not with me is against me

(Pope John Paul and New Age Movement)

In his book, Pope John Paul also attacks the New Age Movement in Europe. He does it in the very chapter in which he attacks Hinduism, Buddhism, Yoga, techniques and methods of meditation, and "*ideas originating in the religious traditions of the Far East.*" This shows what he suspects about this Movement. Let us give it a closer look.[1]

His criticism of it is sharp and he drops all efforts to be polite in dealing with it. The reason is simple. The Movement is the enemy within; it is seditious; it is heretic and deserves no quarters. But thank God, it is not old Europe and the Church's hands are tied.

The Movement is based on no single idea but is made up of various ideas and strands. Those who join it have diverse inspiration, but most of them find the religion and culture of their birth

---

1. Religious commotion in Europe is wide-spread. Those who love statistics and keep track of these things tell us that there are 95 'spirit-movements' in the United Kingdom, 450 in Germany and 500 in the U.S.A. Many of them are Christian —even fanatically Christian. The Seventh Day Adventists and the "Born Again" movement are two examples. The last one is headed by one Sun Myung Moon, a Korean — the only Eastern thing about it. Moon claims that at the age of sixteen he had a vision which told him to complete the unfinished mission of Jesus. Jesus in his life was deserted by John the Baptist and rejected by the people so that he had to die on the cross before his time while his true mission was to marry and to establish the kingdom of heaven on earth. To fulfill this mission, a new messiah had to be born in Korea as Moon.

From this wider movement, the Pope has chosen for his attack only one section, the one which is Hindu-Buddhist in orientation. Why? It is because he knows in his heart that it is the most serious and important part. With the rest, the Church would be able to deal in good time and probably they would themselves peter out. But this section is a serious affair. It has behind it a fundamental system of ideas, an ancient tradition; its opposition is fundamental and its strength does not depend on its numerical count at a particular moment.

narrow and unsatisfying. Many are simply in revolt but some are also looking for new ideas. They have new intuitions about men, Gods and the world around them. They become environmentalists, take to vegetarianism. They seek new sciences, more compassionate ways of living, holistic and non-violent systems of health. Many of them also know something about religions coming from the Far East and find them attractive. They think and write about Tao, Krishna Consciousness, law of karma; they study Hindu-Buddhist scriptures seriously and find in them the truths which their own deeper mind was seeking. No doubt, those who manage Christianity find it disturbing.

The Movement has no name or address. It is not institutionalized; it is diffused; it cannot be pinned down; it is everywhere though it cannot be seen or localized. Therefore it is even more dangerous. The Church rightly suspects it; it does not feel comfortable with anything it does not control.

In this Movement the Pope sees the "*return of ancient gnostic ideas under the guise of the so-called New Age.*" He calls it a new way of practising old "Gnosticism", which he describes in these words: "that attitude of the spirit that, in the name of a profound knowledge of God, results in distorting His Word and replacing it with purely human words." He tells us that "Gnosticism never completely abandoned the realm of Christianity. Instead it has always existed side by side with Christianity, sometimes taking the shape of a philosophical movement, but more often assuming the characteristics of a religion or para-religion in distinct, if not declared, conflict with all that is essentially Christian."

Thus if we are to believe the Pope, the New Age Movement is not a thing of today or yesterday but has a long ancestry; it is also not ad hoc but has links with larger ideas, and ultimately it has its sources in Eastern religions. Such a Movement deserves better respect in its own and in our eyes. Let us have a look at it and discuss it more fully.

Early Gnosticism

It seems Gnosticism had considerable literature at one time before it was destroyed by the Church. In 1945, fifty-two Gnostic texts were discovered near Nag Hammadi by a shepherd, Muhammad Ali, in Upper Egypt. When it was realized how precious the findings were, the whole thing got into legal tangle and their publication was delayed. Now Dr. Elaine Pagels has translated them and they were published under the title *The Gnostic Gospels* by Harper and Row in 1977. They throw light on the earliest period of Christianity, when its dogmas, rites and structure were yet in the making. They tell us of the earliest controversies inside the Church. Everything which seems so settled about the life and death of Jesus was once questioned: his Passion, Crucifixion, Resurrection. Even the Biblical God was under attack; the efficacy of Church rites, and its authority were denied.

The texts shatter the picture of an imagined earlier Christianity which was simpler, purer and more unanimous. Facts show that it was even more disunited than it is today. Today, all forms of Christianity agree on most primary things; they more or less agree on the canon of the New Testament; they confess more or less the same Apostolic Creed. But in the early days, they disagreed on almost every thing. There was no such thing as a fixed canon — many books served this role. A fixed creed, the historicity of Jesus, his being a begotten Son of God, his suffering, death and bodily resurrection — all these were established after a long, bitter and bloody struggle.

To start with, Christianity was Judaic but as it tried to enter the Gentile world, it sought a new idiom. It made an alliance with Gnosticism which, in one form or another, was the real religion of the Graeco-Roman elite. It tried to give Christian apocalyptical beliefs a deeper meaning. Christianity gained immensely from this alliance.

But the alliance soon broke down. The soul of Christianity

was apocalyptical, millennial, historical, and literalist. Gnosticism was spiritual, and philosophical. The genius of orthodox Christianity was organizational; the message of Gnosticism was subversive of any authority. The alliance turned into a bitter inner struggle. The Gnostics were denounced as heretics. After the conversion of Emperor Constantine, Christianity became an official religion in the fourth century, and the Gnostic books were banned and destroyed. Athanasius, the powerful Archbishop of Alexandria, sent out orders in 367 A.D. for purging all apocryphal books with heretical tendencies. Perhaps it was at this time that some monk hid these Gnostic texts in a jar and buried it where they were found after 1600 years.

The work of destruction was so thorough that up till now we knew about the Gnostics only through their detractors and opponents.

The Gnostics were called "monachos" or monks as in the *Gospel of Thomas*. The word "gnosis" (Skt. *jñana*) means knowledge obtained supernaturally. The Gnostics lived solitary lives and sought mystical enlightenment through reflection and ascetic self-discipline. They taught the ascent of the soul till it unites with *Pleroma,* the fullness of being, the *pūrṇam* of the Upanishads. The terminology of many of the Gnostic texts is Jewish, but their philosophy is Platonic, Hermetic and, directly or indirectly, Hindu. Bardesanes, the last of the Gnostics, was confessedly influenced by his acquaintance with Hindu thought. Hippolytus includes Brahmanism as a source of Gnostic heresy. He says that there is "among the Indians a heresy of those who philosophize among the Brahmins, who live a self-sufficient life, abstaining from eating living creatures and all cooked food...They say that God is light, not like the light one sees, nor like the sun nor fire [*Kaṭhopanishad* 2-2-15], but to them God is discourse [*Vāk, Praṇava*], not that which finds expression in articulate sounds, but that of knowledge (*gnosis*), through which the secret mysteries of nature are perceived by the wise."

Man and God

The affinity between Gnosticism and Hindu thought is closer than has been yet recognized. Semitic orthodoxy says that God is wholly the other, though he is shown with all the passions of man; the Gnostics along with the Vedantins hold that the seeker and the sought are at heart one and their nature is spiritual; that the Self and the Divine are identical; and that Self-knowledge is the true knowledge of God. Montanus declared: "I am the Father, the Word, and the Paraclete." It created problems not merely of theology but of political authority too. The situation was further complicated by the fact that his morals were blameless. He was excommunicated in 175 and his followers were completely suppressed by Emperor Justinian (483-565 A.D.).

Like the Hindus, the Gnostics speak not of sin and repentance but of illusion (*avidyā*) and enlightenment (*bodhi*). Both conceive God not merely as a father but also as a mother. According to both, the true teacher resides in the heart, and when the pupil also knows, he becomes as good as the teacher.

With such a different fundamental framework, there is no wonder that the Gnostics differed with the Catholics on most questions. In the long history of he Church, it has known much criticism, but never did it emanate from so fundamentally a different perspective.

The texts could be studied from various angles, but Elaine Pagels shows us how Gnostic forms of Christianity interacted with orthodoxy, and how their mutual debate helped to make the Church dogmas and shape Church power-structure. She shows that these bitter debates were not merely religious but involved questions of power and authority. Behind theological terminology were political motivations and nuances.

Jesus's Suffering

The two parties differed completely on this question. To the Catholics, the suffering and death of Jesus on the cross were real;

to the Gnostics, they were more apparent than real. According to them, Jesus had a spiritual nature which did not suffer on the cross, nor it knew death. *The Acts of John* says that Jesus, in so far as he was the son of man, suffered and died; but in so far as he was the Son of God, he neither suffered, nor died. It is close to the Upanishadic teaching of two birds on a tree, one of which eats, enjoys and suffers and the other merely looks on (*Śvetāśvatara Upanishad* 4.6-7).

A bitter controversy ensued. Pope Leo I (447 A.D.) condemned writings like the *Acts of John* as "a hotbed of manifold perversity" which "should not only be forbidden but entirely destroyed and burnt with fire." The Nicene Council directed that "no one is to copy this book; not only so, but we consider that it deserves to be consigned to the fire."

Why so much heat and bitterness? Elaine Pagels says that at the back of its theology, the question had an eminently practical side. She says that during the early period of Christianity when it suffered a measure of persecution, the Church officials encouraged martyrdom. They asked their followers "to imitate the passion of Jesus Christ." But if his suffering was unreal, then their lives were just thrown away. "In that case, I am dying in vain," Ignatius, the Bishop of Antioch, argued. Martyrdom had meaning only if Jesus "was truly persecuted under Pontius Pilate, was truly crucified, and died," he added.

Martyrdom

Martyrdom itself was not highly thought of by many Gnostics. According to them, the deluded martyrs were mistaken in thinking that Jesus shared their kind of mortality and that martyrdom could bring them salvation. "These empty martyrs" bear witness to no truth but "they bear witness only to themselves," says *The Testimony of Truth*. These morbid exhibitionists and misguided enthusiasts did not know "who Christ is" (*The Second Apocalypse of James*). Another Gnostic teacher, Heracleon, did not reject martyrdom altogether but preached that a Gnostic witness to Christ is superior to a martyr's "blood witness." Only such gnosis is true martyrdom and true testimony. The Gnostics condemned the Church functionaries who coerced innocent believers "to the executioner" and encouraged the "little ones" to embrace martyrdom in order to win cheap popularity for themselves and their Church.

The orthodox were angered. Irenaeus threatened that "all who have cast a slur upon their martyrs shall be confounded by Christ."

Baptism

Gnostics did not believe in Baptism, the sacred rite of the Catholics. According to them, baptism did not make a Christian. The *Gospel of Philip* says that many people "go down into the water and come up without having received anything."

Resurrection

The bodily resurrection of Jesus was also a point of heated controversy. Resurrection to the Gnostics was spiritual, to the orthodox corporeal. The former considered the literal view of resurrection as the "faith of the fools." According to them, those who talk of the bodily resurrection are "dealers in bodies"; they proclaim "a doctrine of a dead man" *(The Second Treatise of the Great Seth)*. To them, the experience of enlightenment alone was true "resurrection" (*The Testimony of Truth*). To them, resurrection was not something that happened to some particular man in the past; it is a continuing phenomenon. "Those who say they will die first and then rise are in error"; instead, they must "receive the resurrection while they live," says the *Gospel of Philip*. This echoes the Upanishadic teaching: "We may know This while we are here... Those who know this become immortal, but others go only to sorrow" (*Brihadāraṇyaka Upanishad* 4.4.14).

But the orthodox school stuck to its guns. Tertullian (190 A.D.)

said that what was raised was "this flesh, suffused with blood, built up with bones, interwoven with nerves, entwined with veins." If this proposition looks absurd, "it must be believed, because it is absurd," i.e. lie to yourself stubbornly. Out of this passionate controversy came the future dogmas that Jesus "truly suffered, was crucified, dead and buried," and "did truly rise again from death, and took again his body, with flesh, bones..."

Elaine Pagels says that this was too at heart a political question. Both parties agreed that Jesus Christ had the authority.[2] But who was to administer this authority? The Gnostics said anyone who became spiritually alive, who came into contact with the "living god." Such a doctrine is subversive of all authority. The orthodox said that the authority belonged to the Apostles, who first saw Jesus bodily risen from the dead. "All power is given unto me in heaven and in earth," the risen Jesus told the eleven disciples and delegated this power to them. It was a cosmic transfer of authority, first from God to Jesus, then from Jesus to the eleven Apostles, particularly to Peter to whom Jesus said, "Feed my Sheep."

According to the Church tradition (though not supported by the gospels), Peter was "the first witness of the resurrection" (according to most gospels, it was Mary Magdalene but being a woman she did not matter), and, therefore, the rightful claimant to the chieftainship of the Church. The authority now belonged to Peter's Church and his successors from generation to generation.

God

The concept of God is important in all theologies, but though they use this word, they mean very different things by it. The

2. Some Gnostics (who later came to be known as Christian Gnostics) made the initial mistake of entertaining *Jesus* in their theology; and though they explained him as *Christ* and gave him a non-historical meaning but it was bound to create confusion in the long run. It became their weak point, their Achilles' heel. They were eventually overpowered by their rivals whose creed was centred on a purely historical figure, Jesus, and not on a non-historical truth or principle — man's inner divinity.

Gnostics tried to give a deeper meaning to the Biblical God; some rejected him altogether and called him an "accursed god", the "malicious envier" whose tyranny the serpent (the symbol of divine wisdom) taught Adam and Eve to resist. They called Jehovah (more correctly Yahweh) "malevolent", "blind", "arrogant", "foolish", and "ignorant."

The Gnostics on their part taught a "God beyond God" and called him the "abyss", the "ground of being." Like the *Brahma* of the Upanishads, they described him negatively (*neti neti*) as "invisible, and incomprehensible." Self-knowledge is the basis of God-knowledge. "....Whoever has not known himself has known nothing, but he who has known himself has at the same time already achieved knowledge about the depths of all things" (*The Book of Thomas the Contender*). One Gnostic teacher, Simon Magus, says that in each man "dwells an infinite power", which is also "the root of the universe." By knowing the Self, all this is known (*idam sarvam viditam, Brihadāraṇyaka Upanishad* 4.5.6).

The Upanishads teach that you become what you know. The *Gospel of Philip* repeats this teaching: "You saw the spirit, you shall become spirit... You saw the Father, you shall become the Father... You see yourself, and what you see, you shall become."

The Politics of Monotheism

Elaine Pagels tell us that the question of One, Sole God was a political question for the Catholics. The theology of One God in heaven supported the politics of One Bishop on the earth. The earth mirrors the heaven. Here on the earth, the bishop presides "in the place of God." Ignatius tells the laity to obey the bishop "as if he were God."

Church Authority

In fact, the Gnostics repudiated the whole concept of the Church and its claim to authority. They distinguished between the "visible" Church of the common clergy, and the real, "invisible"

Church of those who live in holiness, or in the "rational brotherhood of wisdom." The visible Church is only an "imitation Church." *The Apocalypse of Peter* calls Church dignitaries the "messengers of error." Obedience to them is to submit oneself to "blind guides." But the orthodox taught just the opposite. For them the Catholic Church under the bishop is "the entrance to life; all others are thieves and robbers.' Ignatius says that "to join with the bishop is to join the Church; to separate oneself from the bishop is to separate oneself not only from the Church, but from God himself." Thus God was identified with the Church and the Church with the bishop.

Salvation: Self-knowledge

Echoing the Upanishadic thought, the Gnostics preached that salvation comes "when the man knows himself" (*The Testimony of Truth*). The word for salvation they used was *apolytrosis,* literally *release*, a close translation of *moksha*.

But the orthodox on the other hand followed the lead of Paul who taught that even if "an angel from heaven, preach any other gospel...let him be accursed" (Gal I.8). The Gnostics said that this was no proper attitude for learning. Jesus taught to seek and knock (Mat 7.7). The soul longs to "see with her mind, and perceive her kinsmen, and learn about her roots," they said. But the Christian followers are merely taught to believe; these are "the ones who are ignorant, who do not seek after God," they said.

Tertullian answered on behalf of the orthodox. "We want no curious disputation after possessing Jesus Christ, no inquiring after enjoying the gospel," he said. And again: "Away with the person who is seeking where he never finds." He is here referring to any seeking outside of the fold of the Church, which is in vain, according to the orthodox viewpoint.

True Saviour and Teacher

The figure of *Soter* is anterior to Christianity. In many Gnostic works, the figure of the redeemer is entirely absent, in others he plays little historical role. The canonical *Gospel of St. John* makes Jesus say, "I am the Way...no one comes to the Father, but by me." But the *Gospel of Thomas,* a Gnostic work, provides a different answer: "There is light within a man of light, and it lights up the whole world. If he does not shine, he is in darkness." A man is his own saviour.

Similarly, he is also his own teacher. There is no permanent, third-person teacher in the shape of a historical Jesus, a teacher *par excellence* for all times gone and to come. The seeker is a "disciple of his own mind"; and his mind "is the father of the Truth," says *The Testimony of Truth.* "Live according to your mind...light the lamp within you," says Silvanus, a Gnostic teacher. It is the same as the Buddha's advice to a seeker to be his own lamp, or the Gita's teaching to realize the Self by the Self. For he who seeks is also the one who reveals. There is also no permanent gulf between the pupil and the teacher. Once the pupil "knows", both become equal. To a disciple who also comes to "realize," Jesus tells, "I am not your teacher" (*Gospel of Thomas*).

Woman

The Old Testament God whom the Christians worshipped was conceived only as the Father, but to the Gnostics, the ultimate principle was also conceived as the Mother. According to Valentinus (140 A.D.), a great Gnostic teacher, God is Ineffable, the Depth, the Primal Father; but he is also the Grace, the Silence, the Womb and "Mother of All." The Gnostics quoted the Genesis to say that God created man in his own image...male and female created he them"; and argued that God, therefore, must be *androgynous*, both male and female, like the *Ardhanārīśvara* of the Hindus.

Theology is also anthropology. Because woman had a place of honour in the Gnostic pantheon, she had also an honourable place in their worldly affairs. She participated on equal terms in all their gatherings and cultures. Tertullian thunders against "these heretical women" and tells us "how audacious they are! They have no modesty; they are bold enough to teach, to engage in argument, to enact exorcisms, to undertake cures, and, it may be, even to baptize!"

On the other hand, woman had hardly any place in the Catholic hierarchy, heavenly or temporal. It followed Paul's lead who said that man is not of the woman, but woman is of the man; and that man was not created for the woman but woman for the man (I Cor 11.7-9). Woman was to keep silent and "learn in silence with all submissiveness" (I Tim 2.11). The old tradition of excluding woman from clerical life still continues, Pope Paul VI declaring in 1977 that a woman cannot be a priest "because our Lord was a man."

Though Christianity regards Gnosticism as an enemy, it owes much to its influence in the early days. Music received recognition in the Church because of Gnostic influence. But unfortunately this influence failed in securing a better place for woman in the Church thinking and organization.

* * * *

The above discussion shows why the Pope regards the New Age Movement with hostility. He regards it as an old enemy. If it derives from old Gnosticism as the Pope believes and as it seems to do, then it is easy to understand his hostility. The Movement is subversive of Christianity — its ideas, its externality, its exclusiveness, its authoritarianism. Quite understandably, other evangelical denominations and all those who are managing Christianity share this attitude of hostility. In their new book, *Satan's Evangelistic Strategy for This New Age*, E. W. Lutzer and J. F. DeVries warn: "America is being converted to a new religion. It is called the New Age Movement. It comes from the age-old lies of Satan himself." In the Movement itself they see "the influence of Eastern Religions," which "best represent the lies of Eden." They say that the Devil does not "expect Americans to become Hindus" right away, but his strategy for the time being is to take them "beyond the one true God and His Son, Jesus Christ." The authors are especially critical of pantheism, *karma*, rebirth, Yoga and other ideas connected with Hinduism and Buddhism.

Terry Muck, the editor of *Christianity Today*, sounds a similar warning in his *Alien Gods on American Turf.* He speaks of "the invisible crisis" in Christianity. He warns that "ten or twenty years from now, the full force of non-Christian religion will be felt... Currently we have no philosophy or theology that adequately deals with the presence of the world religions in our midst."

Pat Robertson whom we have already met (p.12) says that the New Age, as it is in America, and Hinduism — "it's the same thing." Both are based on karma, on rebirth or reincarnation, on cycle of life. "The whole thought of your karma, of meditation ... this is all Hinduism," he says. He warns: "We're importing Hinduism into America ... We can't let that stuff come into America. We've got the best defence, if you will — a good offense."

All this shows that the Movement has a great responsibility to shoulder and a great role to play — an old role in a new context. To play it adequately and honourably, it has to become more conscious of its inspiration, its underlying ideas and philosophy; it has to become aware of its lost Pagan ancestry, its Eastern links and its common spiritual heritage.

4
Dislike of Alikes
(Pope John Paul on Judaism and Islam)

After disposing of Eastern religions and the New Age Movement, Pope John Paul comes to Judaism and Islam, the "great monotheistic religions", and to "synagogues and mosques, where those who worship the One God assemble." It is a subject with which he is on familiar grounds and which is close to Christianity doctrinally.

Judaism

He speaks softly about Judaism and the Jews, a new fashion imposed by new intellectual conditions. He tells the Jews that the "New Covenant has its roots in the Old," and calls them "our elder brothers in faith." He refers to the Second Vatican Council which says that "in God's plan of salvation", the beginning of Church's faith and election "is to be found in the Patriarchs, Moses and the Prophets"; which recalls Paul's words that to the Israelites "belong the sonship, the glory, the covenants, the giving of the law, the worship, and the promises"; it recalls that "the apostles, the pillars on which the Church stands, are of Jewish descent."

The Pope further assures the Jews that Christianity has been carrying forward the work of Judaism and has served "to fulfil all that is rooted in the vocation of Abraham, in God's covenant with Israel at Sinai, and in the whole rich heritage of the inspired Prophets." He reminds them how Jesus, the Son of God, was "according to the flesh, also the son of Israel" — a painful reminder though, for they know they were cursed in this son and he brought them a future of misery and tribulation.

But is this sincere and will it suffice? Will it undo what has continued to be done to the Jews for 2000 years, of which the recent Nazi atrocities were only one extreme instance? Not likely, for the supporting religious ideology remains intact. The Pope continues to insist that the Jews must not trust their own inspiration but eventually come to God through Jesus and that Judaism can find its fulfillment only in Christianity. He awaits the time "when the people of the Old Covenant will be able to see themselves as part of the New", though for the time being he is leaving the question of its fulfillment "to the Holy Spirit." In the past, the Spirit has worked best when its work was facilitated by "salutary severity", by Inquisition and mob threat.[1]

Islam

From very early days, Christianity and Islam have had a love-hate relationship. The two ideologies have much in common doctrinally and have a great psychic affinity. They have no idea of a larger humanity and divide humanity into *us* and *they*, into *believers* and *unbelievers*, *mu'mins* and *kāfirs*. But these similarities have not stopped them from being at loggerheads for the better part of history. However, for the present, the Pope speaks of Islam in polite words. Quoting the Second Vatican Council, he says that the "Church has a high regard for the Muslims who worship one God", who though not acknowledging Jesus as God "worship him as a prophet", who also honour the Virgin Mother Mary. He also proffers his own regards and assures that "Believers in Allah are particularly close to us."

---

1. For example, we learn that St. Vincet Ferrer (d. 1419 A.D.), a Dominican, urged the Jews to convert while the Christian mobs zealously aided his pleading by massacring those who hesitated. As a result, thousands of Jews were converted, and those who relapsed were imprisoned and burned by the Inquisition. It was discovered that no less than 17,000 of the Saint's converts had returned to Judaism, and were dealt with according to the Christian law of apostasy.

It is politer than anything said before. Till yesterday, Christianity regarded Islam as a "spurious faith", and its prophet as "false", "wicked", and "licentious", though Islam was also welcome for being a scourge of idolators — their common name for the rest of humanity. But now Pope John Paul's approach is more conciliatory. First, because Christianity has lost much of its old power on its own turf; secondly, because Islam is no longer poor and powerless. The Church now pleads with all concerned "to forget the past, and urges that a sincere effort be made to achieve mutual understanding," to put it in the language of the Second Vatican Council.

The need to forge mutual understanding, however, does not prevent the Pope from playing ideological sleight of hand. Saying one thing while meaning another, he states that "*the religiosity of Muslims deserves respect.*" It is his way of saying that while Muslims are religious, Islam is *not* a religion. Whether true or not, it would not flatter Muslims and win them over.[2]

Speaking more plainly, the Pope points out how and where Christianity differs from Islam. First, he says that "*Islam is not a religion of redemption.* There is no room for the Cross and the Resurrection. Jesus is mentioned, but only as a prophet, who prepares for the last prophet, Muhammad. There is also mention of Mary, His Virgin Mother, but the tragedy of redemption is completely absent. For this reason not only the theology but also the anthropology of Islam is very distant from Christianity."

---

2. The Christian strategists have adopted this new line with all other religions. For example, Hindus too are praised by them for their "uncommon spiritual gift", their "unquenchable thirst for whatever is spiritual", their "deep interiority" which has led even many Christians to "deepen their own interiority"; but the ultimate truth, however, lies with the Church. "India has to receive humbly from the Church the sound and basic principles of true contemplation... built on the unshakable foundation of revealed truths concerning God and men and their mutual relations," says pompously the late Fr. J. Monchanin, who was a diehard missionary but who assumed the name and dress of a Hindu sannyasin.

A Reduced Revelation

Continuing, the Pope says that "in Islam all the richness of God's self-revelation, which constitutes the heritage of the Old and New Testaments, has definitely been set aside." In conclusion, he says that anyone who reads the Bible and then the Quran can clearly see the process by which Islam "*completely reduces Divine Revelation.*"

But how it was done and how it could be done at all, the Pope does not elucidate. When Islam received the older Revelation, it was reduced enough and it is not clear how it could be reduced further. Looked at superficially, the two Revelations may differ here and there, but to a deeper look they are very much alike both historically as well as in their basic ideation; they differ as tweedledum from tweedledee and it is difficult to see how one could be a reduced version of the other. Allah is a good copy of Jehovah and does not suffer in comparison.

The point becomes clearer if we look at the three revelatory religions historically. Judaism, the parent religion, was a religion of the *ummah* par excellence. Its God had adopted a special people and those people had adopted a special God. According to their agreement, the people were to worship him alone and he was to exalt them above all nations. Then came Christianity which embraced the Judaic God but denied his people. But it is doubtful whether God also did it and agreed to adopt a new people, though Christianity claims that he did. When Islam came, the old story was repeated though in a low key. Islam silently embraced the Judaic God and the Judaic prophets but dropped the Jews.

In all this adoption of old God and new people, we notice one thing: there is no concept of mankind and no concept of a universal God. Probably there was nothing wrong in this so long as the special God and special people were not bellicose. But it was not to be so. The God of the Jews claimed some sort of primacy and sovereignty over all but in practice he was satisfied by the worship of his chosen people, and he did not care about others. The case, however, was different when he was adopted by Christians and Muslims. He now sought a different kind of primacy; he wanted to become the God of all through conquest and slaughter. And that is the universality this special God has known most of the time.

Reduced Spirituality

Probably it could be argued that since man has lived in groups, he could not think of a universal God. But this is wrong perception. Though man lives physically in groupings, he is endowed with a universal and even cosmic dimension in his intellectual conception and in his spiritual and ethical sensibility. For example, the Greeks who like all other people also lived as a sub-group and were even proud Hellenists had no difficult in this regard. Like other Pagan people, wherever they went they were able to find their own Gods in the Gods of others. But the story of revelatory religions is different: wherever they went they found devils in the Gods of others.

The problem of revelatory religions or Revelations is that they represent a reduced spirituality. They have a reduced concept of Godhood, of man, and of their relationship. They have hardly any concept of an "Unknown" and "Unknowable God" (Acts 17.23); they only know a "known God", a God who can be proclaimed and announced from the house-tops.

This God necessarily lacks *internality*. These Revelations have no concept of a God seen in the heart by a purified *buddhi*. Lacking internality, he also lacks true *universality*. He is merely the God of a favoured church or *ummah* and a hater of the rest. He struck a *covenant* with a chosen people from which larger mankind was kept out altogether. Animals, plants, and elements had of course no share in his promise; they were merely for man's use and exploitation. Thus ethics and ecology suffered a great reduction.

Intermediary

And though the God of a chosen people, he refused to reveal himself directly to them. He did it through a favoured buddy. The chosen people must derive their spirituality from this chosen spokesman and be saved by him. God does not reveal himself to them but he insists that they obey him.

The Christian and Islamic Revelations have a low idea of their God, ethically speaking. He is poor in higher ethical qualities. He is an angry god, a jealous god, a god of revenge and spoils (*infāl*); he lacks reason (*logos*) and is known for his arbitrariness; he is not lofty but merely high-handed.

As the two Revelations had a low idea of God, they had also as a result a low idea of man. Man was reduced to a vital-mental dimension; he lost his spiritual dimension. He lost not only *eternal* life but also his evolutionary lives, his capacity for self-formation through many lives. He lived one brief life but was condemned, in most cases, for eternity.

In short, the two Revelations reduced the concept of religion itself. Religion was no longer truth of the spirit; it became a hegemonic ideology, a creed to be imposed by *jihād* and salesmanship. Man's prayer took the form of a dogma, of beliefs, of articles of faith, which could be numbered, catechized, labelled and exported. Religion could be put into a single *kalima*; it could be agitated about and turned into a battle-cry.

To conclude, spirituality was reduced to the minimum in the two Revelations. It was reduced to a narrow form of theism — monotheism; which in turn was reduced to monolatry and prophetry. And the two between them have come to mean a special type of religious ideology — an ideology of one God, one Prophet, one Intermediary or Saviour, one book, one doctrine, one life, and one judgment. They have no concept of Plurality, of the Many, of the Vast — the *bhūmā* of the Upanishads; they have little internality and universality. Reduction has been having a full play.

5

Old half-lies will make one new, whole truth

(Pope John Paul on Christianity)

Pope John Paul discusses Christianity — in fact, that is why the book was written. He goes over all its doctrines and rites and makes all the old claims for them; he discusses ecumenism, the need for all major Christian denominations to come under one flag; he discusses the new problem Christianity now faces, the problem of proselytizing in a world no longer ruled by Christianity.

As expected, the Pope makes pretentious theological claims; he makes claims for Christianity's God, its founder, its Apostles, its Church, its officials, its rites. He repeats the claim that Jesus is the Son of God, that he is the Second Person of the God of the Trinity, that the Church is his Bride, and that the Pope is his Vicar on earth. He says that Jesus is unique — "*totally original and unique,*" he insists. He is not just "a wise man like Socrates", or "enlightened like Buddha"; he is "*the one mediator between God and humanity,*" the Pope adds repeating the Church dogma. Jesus is the saviour, the only saviour of man naturally and helplessly condemned to be sinful.[1]

---

1. Sin and saviour are related ideas. One reinforces the need of the other. Sinful men need a saviour; and a saviour needs sinners. Luther also solved the problem in another and a novel but psychologically significant way — by giving a sinful man a sinful saviour. He tells us that "Christ committed adultery first of all with the woman at the well... Secondly with Mary Magdalene, and thirdly with the woman taken in adultery..." (*Table Talk*, 1472, quoted by Peter F. Wiener in his *Martin Luther*). He says the same about the Christian saints and apostles. "The Saints must be good, downright sinners." "The Apostles themselves were sinners, yea, regular scoundrels... I believe that the prophets also frequently sinned grievously." It is so reassuirng to the sinful man that if he is not like his saviour, his saviour is like him. It is *Advaita* in reverse. If one cannot be like one's God, one's God is like him.

In exalting Jesus, the Pope however does not forget Mary. We all know how at one stage she eclipsed even Jesus and became the supreme object of worship. During Medieval Ages, Mary was the real mediator in real practice — "supreme intercessor", even "co-redeemer of the human race", as she was called. In any case, she became the intercessor or mediator between Jesus and the believers, and Jesus himself tended to become redundant. Theology had already become Christology, but now it became Mariology. Pope John Paul explains that a "*Marian dimension and Mariology in the Church are simply another aspect of the Christological focus.*" But it did not happen without much controversy. Many lovers of Jesus yielded gladly to her claim since it was still in the family and it was another way of honouring Jesus. Also those who could believe in one mediator could as well believe in one more. But the more doctrinaire elements — they were one-Godist as well as one-Saviourist — did not yield and the controversy has continued in one form or another. Protestants have often called Mary a "witch."

But now the cult of Mary is experiencing difficulty from another source. It is not on account of her being an additional god-figure, but on account of her being a virgin and a mother. Motherhood and virginity are not particularly creditable these days. The Church is fighting to retain the figure of a virgin and mother Mary against great odds. Let us hope it succeeds.

The Pope on himself

John Paul is not averse to making claims about himself too. To the question, whether he is the Vicar of Christ, his answer is somewhat convoluted but clear. He says he is not afraid "when people call me the Vicar of Christ, when they say to me Holy Father, or Your Holiness." It is somewhat of a climb down. In another age, it would have been others who had to be really afraid for not calling him Vicar of Christ, etc. But now times have changed and a Pope has to be bold to wear those titles. Perhaps in his own person John

Paul may be a modest man, but with all the theologies telling him he is infallible, his cough has to be loud.

The Source of Grace and Teaching

The Church has always claimed that it is the sole vehicle of grace and salvation.[2] In the past, it said it plump out, but now it has to indulge in some hedging. The Second Vatican Council repeats and the Pope reiterates the old position as best as they can under the circumstances. The Council says that the Church's vocation is to teach, that it "is missionary by her very nature"; that it sets men "free from the slavery of error and incorporates them into Christ"; that it works "for the glory of God, the confusion of the Devil and the happiness of man." John Paul repeats all these claims and says that for any man "to hope for salvation from God", he "must stop beneath Christ's Cross."

Church Rites

The Pope also makes claims for the Church sacraments and rites like baptism[3] and eucharist.[4] He says that "when the Church bap-

---

2. That the Church is the sole agency of salvation became the dogma of the Church almost as soon as it was born. Bishop Cyprian (d. 248 A.D.) says: "He who has not the Church for his mother, cannot have God for his father." Bishop Augustine (354-430 A.D.), a Church father, says: "He who dies out of the Church is doomed to eternal damnation, even if he were burned alive for the name of Christ."

3. What baptism does is important enough but what happens to those who go unbaptized is even more important. The whole world of unbaptized pagans goes to hell. So do all infants of Christian parents who die before baptism. It sounds cruel but all early Church fathers agree on this point according to Wall's *History of Infant Baptism.* St. Augustine says that all such infants go to "everlasting fire." St. Fulgentius says that "children who have begun to live in their mothers' womb and have there died, or who, having been just born, have passed away from the world without the sacrament of holy baptism... must be punished by the eternal torture of undying fire." St. Thomas Aquinas was somewhat more considerate about an infant who dies in the womb: "God may have ways of saving it for aught we know."

The Church's opposition to abortion has been on the ground of the undelivered babies' souls who remaining unbaptized go to hell. But now there

tizes, it is Christ who baptizes; when the Church absolves, it is Christ who absolves; when the Church celebrates the Eucharist, it is Christ who celebrates it."

The Pope makes claims for his priests too and says that "Christ brings about a special presence in every priest, who, when celebrating the Eucharist or administering the sacraments, does so in persona Christi."

Hell

In laying forth all these claims, John Paul does not forget the Christian hell. There was a time when the Church had a fertile *eschatological vision* or vision about "*the last things*."[5] Christian

---

seems to be a shift in the viewpoint as the Pope's March, 1995 *evangelium vitae* (doctrine for life) shows. It is a fundamental shift — from the soul to the body. In the past, the Church has not hesitated to burn people's bodies in order to save their souls. Its concern was not *jīva-dayā* (compassion for living beings), it has been more in the line of soul-saving.

Exorcism accompanies baptism. At the ceremony, the priest pronounces: "I exorcise thee, unclean spirit, in the name of Jesus Christ; tremble, O Satan! thou enemy of faith ..." The Devil then departs.

4. Eucharist is another most important sacrament. In this, the performer eats Jesus's flesh and drinks his blood. It is no mere metaphor or symbol according to the Church. It insists that "Christ himself, whole and entire, is *substantially* present" in the consecrated bread. A Jew was converted to the Christian faith; when watching a priest dividing a loaf, he saw a "child being cut limb by limb" and he knew that what was "given him was flesh indeed." Such stories have often been cited in Catholic circles to provoke faith, but the whole creed is offensive, particularly to Hindu-Buddhist sensibilities. When the Malabar Hindus learnt of this sacrament from B. Ziegenbalg, they found it revolting and said that "none of us will ever be able to comprehend." De Nobili kept its meaning hidden from his converts and told them that the mass was another form of *keertan*.

5. The "last things" in Christianity have no spiritual connotation; it means no special doctrine of death like the one taught by old teachers — *dying before dying*, or to remember death while living and to remember while dying that death is unreal and it is in the nature of a "change of clothes." On the other hand, "last things" in Christian theology are *physical* facts neatly set in time. Early Christianity was expecting the "end of the world" and the "day of judgment" at any moment. The "last things" often began to include other ideas too: like the ideas of an anti-Christ, the second coming, a millennium, a kingdom of Jesus before the day of reckoning and the last judgment. The ideas of devil

scholars know and Pope John Paul assures us that it was an "original, Biblical vision." Uptil recently, Christianity spoke of Hell and Purgatory with great familiarity and also profit, but now these things are "*only faintly present in traditional preaching*," the Pope bemoans. He adds that preachers do not have the "courage to preach the threat of Hell. And perhaps even those who listen to them have stopped being afraid of Hell." He says that *secularization* and *secularism* have produced this "*insensitivity*" and "*eschatology has become irrelevant to contemporary man*." He looks at terrible crimes (and in revelatory religions the most terrible ones are of a theological nature) and asks the question: "Can they go unpunished?" And answering his question by another question he asks whether in the complex history of humanity, "Is not Hell in a certain sense the ultimate safeguard of man's moral conscience?"

In good old days, not long ago, Christianity had no qualms in sending to hell the best of the people belonging to other religions and cultures. But now things have changed. The faith of the faithful has changed and hearing such things is jarring to many ears. Therefore the Church has to present its dogmas in a less offensive way. It now concedes that non-Christian good men are also saved, but it is because in the mystery of God they already belong to "the invisible church." The late Cardinal Jean Danielou relented and said that Buddha and Zoroaster were saved but "they were saved by Christ Who alone saves," he insisted.

---

and hell were intimately related. The final fate of the unsaved souls was a lake of fire and brimstone (Rev 20.10). Christian art painted their torments with great conviction and Christianity came to rule through fear and religious terror of the post-mortal state. Devil was a living presence for believing Christians. He was working overtime tempting pious Christians to commit sins and waiting to snatch their souls and even their bodies to hell. Jules Michelet in his *Satanism and Witchcraft* tell us of a prior in the thirteenth century so terribly afraid of being taken away bodily by the Devil that he had himself guarded day and night by two hundred armed men.

The hotter the fire, the greater the need for a saviour and his Church.

Ecumenism

Christianity is not *one* religion. It seldom was.[6] Its beliefs and rites always divided it. It became one negatively — in opposing others. It first became one in opposition to its Pagan neighbours; then it became one again during the colonial era.

Colonies helped Christian sects to unite in many ways. First, by stressing that the new-found pagans were the common enemy and the missionaries needed to be together. The new lands also provided them unprecedented opportunities. There was a rich crop waiting to be harvested and it needed all the hands. There was enough and to spare for every one. So internal controversies,

---

6. We cannot go here into the question of internal feuds and massacres between different sects and brands of Christianity, how they became competing centres of power, how they fought *national* wars, and how national wars adopted ideological faces. The latest and better known to the average person is between the Catholics and the Protestants. When the Pope excommunicated Luther, he had to take recourse to the language of the Bible (nothing like it when it comes to cursing) and said how the "wild pigs" were trampling down the Church and how the "wild beasts" were feeding on it (Psalm 80.13). Luther often returned the compliments in unprintable terms. Among the Protestants, the Catholic Church is often described by such names as Popery, Scarlet Lady, Whore of Rome, etc.

Mutual quarrels and name-calling among the Protestants were not less sparing. Calvin calls Luther a "half-papist" and his Church a "pig-sty." Calvin in turn had no better reputation among the Lutherans and other Protestants. We are told by them that "Calvin ended his life in despair, with that shameful and loathsome disease (an ulcer in the natural parts), with which God threatens the rebellious and the cursed." The German Lutherans said of him: "God manifested his judgment on Calvin, whom he visited horribly with punishments before his unhappy death; he so struck the heretic, that despairing of salvation, and invoking devils, swearing, and blaspheming he breathed forth his malignant soul." According to the Catholics he was "addicted to shocking immoral practices, and guilty of crimes against nature, he was to have been burnt alive." They are sorry that it was not done and that "after a judicial trial, the sentence was, at the bishop's intercession, commuted into branding, instead of burning." We are told that he was "publicly branded on his back with a fleur-de-lys, in Noyon, his native town." About the Anglican Church, we are told that it was "born in adultery"; Henry VIII, its author, is called "the greatest monster" and Cranmer, his clerical accomplice, is described as "a name which deserves to be held in everlasting execration," by Cobbett, a Protestant writer.

generally about nothing, cooled. The world was divided into spheres of influence. Christian missionaries worked quite amicably in these lands even while Christian nations fought in Europe.

But it does not mean there are no more problems. There is always a struggle for power. For example, the Central and South Americas have been under the domination of the Catholics but now American evangelizers are making a bid there and there is much sheep-stealing. This trespass is resented. The Pope visited these parts recently and speaking in Santo Domingo, Dominican Republic, he said that he had to protect his flock "from the rapacious wolves of evangelical Protestantism" (*Houston Chronicle*, October 13, 1992) — a faithful description of fellow men in the same trade.[7]

In his book, however, the Pope speaks of other Christian denominations with circumspection. They represent important centres of power and they cannot be trifled with. He tells them that what keeps them separate as believers in Christ is much less than what unites them. But this does not stop him from making all the claims for the Catholic Church. He calls it "the body of

---

7. According to the new rivals, Catholic christianization of indigenous peoples in Latin America was "forced and often superficial and the converts are still animists." Similarly, the conversion of Africans (descendents of African slaves settled in the Caribbeans) too was forced. Slaves were baptized as a matter of course before 1804. "Conversion preceded evangelization" and converts continued with many of their old beliefs. As a result much of Catholicism in these parts is really "Woodooism." The new evangelizers say that these people need to be reconverted "to benefit from salvation offered in Jesus Christ." According to Msgr Roberto Luckert, spokesman of the week long Catholic Bishops' Meet at Mexico (Latin America Episcopal Conference), "roughly half of Guatemalans have already converted to Protestant fundamentalism"; he further charges that the new missionaries "are funded by U.S."

What indigenous America and Africa need is not "indigenized Christianity" but recovery of their own old Gods, religions and intuitions. This is a great task waiting to be realized during the next decades. Let us hope they would be able to mobilize enough inner resources to fulfill it. They cannot come into their own and can contribute little to the spiritual movement of mankind without throwing off the yoke of Christianity and Islam.

Christ, a living body which gives life to everything."

World Evangelization

Western arms, prestige and policies have been the greatest factors in recent centuries for the spread of Christianity. But those methods are losing their old importance now. Therefore, the Mission strategists have been discussing other methods of spreading. They have examined world's non-Christian population sector by sector and ideology by ideology to find out what makes some of them unbending, others resistant and yet others relatively pliable. They try to discover "holes" through which these countries could be penetrated more easily. They have also been discussing conditions which favour evangelization. For example, when people are under great mental stress, when they are sick and the doctor and the nurse around are missionaries, they are more prone to missionary influence. Similarly, when people are lonely and lack community life as they do in great cities, or when they are away from their village homes as students in far-away towns, or when they are cut off from their cultural milieu as Asian students are in British and American universities, they are more receptive of a missionary who may be around to befriend them at the moment.

Lausanne Committee for World Evangelization mentions many more conditions favourable to missionary activities. One of them is great political upheavals and socio-cultural changes when people lose confidence in their culture; or some great "cultural dislocation" under which people "become more open to the message of the gospel"; an example is cited of "Kampuchean refugees living in Thai camps, who are becoming Christians in great number." Under similar conditions, insecure and under great pressure and with no one to speak for them, Hindu Namasudras and Buddhist Chakmas of Bangladesh living in camps managed by missionaries are easy targets of their labour.

The Committee also mentions "personal advantage" as a great motivating force. When people believe that "they may advance materially or socially by becoming Christians", they try; which is "true particularly in situations where the missionary is a member of a society that offers educational and material advancement." Similarly, conversion attracts "marginal groups or individuals" who know they can improve "their status in society, as, for example, the Harijans of India."

Pseudo-Marxist radicalism everywhere in Asia has been an intellectual comprador of Western Imperialism. It has aided Imperialism by opposing national movements but its worst role has been in subverting national cultures. It has a very negative view of Hinduism and Buddhism, the deep truths of the human spirit, and the great ideas of the past — and yes of the future too. Therefore, not much good can come out of it. Now Indian left is being used by Christian missionaries in a big way. The missionaries fat with foreign funds are working under many different names and labels; they are active in floating many "voluntary organizations": they are trying to bring intellectuals and social activists together; they are setting up the so-called "human rights" groups which have more often than not been aids and allies of forces working for India's disintegration; they mobilize local "have-nots" against the so-called local "haves" — who are not much of haves except in relative and meaningless sense. The super-rich Christian liberation theologians — so rich that they are even beyond the envy (because beyond the reach) of most of the haves of India — say that it is their Jesus-ordained task to liberate India from social oppression. In the process they have tried to become champions of Indian women, vanavasis and the harijans at no small profit to themselves. True, not many are deceived but they do their best to create mischief. Their aim is to create conditions of disintegration so that they prosper and fish in troubles waters. No doubt they would be defeated. Christianity is inadequate spiritually and it can be no better socially and politically as history proves. Like tree, like fruit.

Missionaries come from diverse denominations but

missiology is one. Pope John Paul shares his strategies with other Christian missions. We have seen what he thinks of other revelatory religions like Judaism and Islam and also what he thinks of great Yogic and pacific religions like Hinduism and Buddhism. The Church has similar strategies with regard to the "animists."[8] The Pope recalls "all the *primitive religions,* the *animistic religions* which stress ancestor worship" without the customary theological shudder. There was a time when animism and ancestor-worship were hated words, but now the Pope finds that "those who practice them are particularly close to Christianity." He finds that ancestor-worship is "a kind of preparation for the Christian faith in the Communion of Saints, in which all believers — whether living or dead — form a single community, a single body" — a single body of which Jesus of course is the head. As a result, he finds there is "nothing strange, then, that the African and Asian animists would become believers in Christ more easily than followers of the *religions of the Far East.*"

Similarly, there is a new revaluation of Chinese Confucianism and Taoism — which were once held in very low esteem as religions. But now the Pope concedes that they "possess the *characteristics of a system*", and that they have "contributed

8. Until recently the word "animist" was under great odium both of theologians as well as anthropologists. Animists were "primitive", "savages", "ancestor-worshippers", "fetishists", "niggers" and "cannibals". Following Biblical lead, Christian Europe believed that they belonged to the cursed tribes of Ham — "Cursed be Canaan; a servant of servants shall he be unto his brethren" (Gen 9.25). Related to it was another tradition that Adam was white while Eve was black. Europe's literature followed the lead of its theology. In Shakespeare's *The Tempest,* Caliban is "a savage and deformed slave", hardly human though Christian Prospero can still manage to recognize in him a "human shape." He is by nature vicious who "any print of goodness will not take. Being capable of all ill." He is ungrateful though Miranda, the Christian daughter, still uses him with "human care." She takes pity on him and even teaches him how to speak but the man just "gabble like a thing most brutish." Caliban understands no higher law of action and "him only stripes may move, not kindness." He, however, has his use for his Christian masters and would "make them fire, and fetch in their wood."

greatly to the history of morality and culture, forming a national identity in the Chinese, Indians, Japanese, and Tibetans, and also in the people of Southeast Asia and the Archipelagoes of the Pacific Ocean."

In the new expansive mood, he also concedes that "some of these people come from age-old cultures." For example, the "indigenous peoples of Australia boast a history of tens of thousands of years old, and their ethnic and religious tradition is older than that of Abraham and Moses." Yet they must accept the tutelage of the younger and junior Jesus for he "came into the world for all these people. He redeemed them all and has His own ways of reaching each of them in the present eschatological phase of salvation history" — assisted by Mrs. Church, His spouse.

More Craft than Courtesy

Today, the Church does not pour venom on non-Christian religions as freely and in the same style as it did before; now its new official line is that "the Catholic Church rejects nothing that is true and holy in those religion"— though it is another matter and a sad commentary on Christianity that in the last 1900 years it has found nothing true and holy in other religions. But if you bring up this point, the Christian apologists think you are unreasonable and even feel persecuted. They throw these words of the Vatican Council in your face and think that they should be enough for you.

However, the concession is withdrawn as soon as it is made, for in the very next sentence the Vatican Council says: "The Church proclaims and is duty bound to proclaim without fail, Christ who is the way, the truth and the life"; and that in him alone "men find the fullness of their religious life." Declaring it quite as pompously, the Pope said during his visit to South America in 1992 that the mission of the Church "is to preach the gospel and give the chance of eternal life to everyone." As a good shepherd, the Church must go on increasing its flock and should not relax on the proselytizing front.

Holy Stubbornness

Throughout his book, Pope John Paul speaks of the problems connected with evangelization and proselytizing. He is aware of the difficulties particularly in this post-colonial period when Christianity does not enjoy the same old political power and prestige. But it would not make him relax. He speaks of the "holy stubbornness" (everything in the Church is holy including Inquisition); he believes that the world already belongs to the Church and it must claim it boldly; he quotes Luke (12.32) where Jesus asks his "little flock" not to be afraid and where "your Father is pleased to give you the Kingdom." Telling them to be courageous, he reminds the missionaries of Jesus that "*the gospel is not a promise of easy success*." At the end, he gives the call for "A great Relaunching of Evangelization."

All this shows that there is only a change of tactics, not of larger aims, that the so-called new Vatican line is not a serious thing, that the conciliatory words said about other religions are a pretence, that they do not mean the end of an old era but the beginning of a new onslaught under different slogans and labels. The fine words are deceptive and it is an ill sign to see a fox lick a lamb.

Christian Theology

John Paul's book belongs to Christian apologetics, a discipline developed to prove and propagate Christian dogmas and attack other religions in their name. It is not concerned with finding the truth. The Church already has the truth, the problem is to propagate it through every means. The Christian theological approach to deeper questions is simplicity itself. It says that Jesus is the Son of God — not in any general sense but literally and exclusively, "the only Begotten Son of God as the Christian creed insists"; that man is sinful and ordinarily beyond redemption, but could be redeemed by a sacrifice as great as his sin. Jesus made this sacrifice by dying. Theologians argue that it shows how great is God's love for man that he sacrificed the life of his only son for man's sake.

It could be argued differently as well. The sacrifice does not show God's love for man, but his hatred for his son — his fear of being replaced by the son, a Freudian would add. But we do not want to enter into this kind of argument. Both are foolish and unspiritual; they give human passions to God and judge him by unregenerate standards.

What is, however, intriguing about the above is how the Christian theologians know all these things. If they knew about themselves even a fraction of what they claim to know about God and his Sons and Grandsons and his purpose and plan in history, they would have done very much less mischief.

It will take a lot of believing to believe that Jesus was the Begotten Son of God, or that Mary was the Virgin Mother of God. Do the Christian theologians really believe it — they who are otherwise so cynical, particularly when they discuss other faiths? Most unlikely. But probably they are like those who say things which are not true in the hope that if they keep on saying them long enough they will become true or at least believable and believed by others. Or perhaps they believe that if they take some old lies or half-lies or half-truths — dependable and time-tested — and put them together in a more acceptable format, they will make one new, whole truth, or at least one wholesome truth.

Religious and Intellectual Liberty

Religious liberty is a new thing in Europe, and it is a hard-earned acquisition. Christianity has been a dealer in truth and Christians had no liberty to make a mistake or to err after the truth was declared by the Church.[9] Persecution of views other

9. St. Augustine says: "What is more deadly to the soul than the liberty of error?" Therefore, about heretic books, he said: "What sane man would permit poison to be publicly scattered about and sold?"

than its own has been the soul of Christianity throughout its long career. It is true of all its denominations. All sections and sects demanded religious toleration and liberty for themselves but denied it to others. Some people think that Reformation brought tolerance and liberty of conscience but it did nothing of the kind. These things came very much later; they came with the triumph of rationalism. The religious wars were not for the cause of freedom, but for establishing the truth of particular sets of doctrines. In these wars, the whole absurdity of Christian dogmatic approach was coming to the fore. In his *A History of Freedom of Thought*, J. B. Bury says that Reformation was as hostile to enlightenment as it was to liberty, and science, if it seemed to contradict the Bible, had as little chance with Luther as with the Pope. Luther described reason as "the devil's appointed whore; whore eaten by scab and leprosy who ought to be trodden under foot and destroyed."

Science subverts Christianity

Liberty to think freely caused havoc to Christianity. It encouraged critical studies of the Bible which revealed that accounts of the Bible are contradictory, that it contains many interpolations, that it has known many versions and its language has differed at a thousand points in these versions, and that, therefore, it could not be the unalterable word of God as it was believed about it.

Freedom of thought also brought about new developments in sciences. That too subverted the authority of the Bible. Developments in astronomy gave Europe new vision of time and space and the earth. So did developments in other fields of natural science. Buffon's *Natural History* (1749 A.D.) showed that the earth was older than what the Bible said. Lyell's *Principles of Geology* (1830 A.D.) and later his *Antiquity of Man* shook the infallibility of the Bible. Darwin's *Origin of Species* (1859) and his *Descent of Man* (1871) "relieved" God of the "labour of creation" as Christianity imagined it. Adam and Eve and the Garden of Eden could be poetry but no longer history as all Europe believed at that time. The development of Anthropology worked in the same direction.[10] As the knowledge of early Christianity increased, it was found that many of its beliefs and rites were not unique to it but were shared by others as well. The Bible was no longer the Word of God and Christian beliefs no longer unique and God-given, but social and political phenomena subject to evolutionary changes.

The Christian ideology was badly undermined. In December 1864, Pope Pius IX issued his Syllabus (*Syllabus Errorum*) condemning 80 "principal errors of our age." It was the most important document of the First Vatican Council (1869-70 A.D.). According to it, all current values of Europe — science, liberty of conscience and opinion, freedom of thought, tolerance — were denounced as heresies. Some of these errors were: that every man is free to adopt and profess the religion he considers true according to the light of reason; that the Church has no right to employ force; that Catholic States should allow foreign immigrants to exercise

10. Anthropology in its origin was colonial in orientation and still is. It applied to Pagan, non-European and non-Christian religions only and it was shown that they were were "primitive", that they derived from lower forms, that they were mythological and superstitious and lacked moral and intellectual contents. Its interpretative method was rarely extended to Christianity as the works of James George Frazer amply show. While other religions and cultures were being treated anthropologically, Christianity continued to be treated theologically — a "whole" made up of ethics and metaphysics and gifted to man from above in a single revelation. In his *Christianity and Mythology*, John M. Robertson makes this interesting observation: "In its treatment of 'pagan' myth the aim is always to go back to the earliest forms, to ignore their symbolical development and later ethical connotations: in the treatment of Christianity the principle is to pass over the concrete myth forms altogether and consider only the metaphysics and ethics that have been grafted on them; or to admit as myths only the Catholic inventions of the Medieval Ages."

But in spite of all the care and caution, the method had a spill-over and began to be applied here and there to Christianity as well. What was said about other religions began to be suspected about Christianity too. For example, some people began to see in eucharist the celebration of an old practice of cannibalism.

their own religion in public. The Syllabus also castigated "indifferentism", that "pernicious doctrine" according to which "eternal salvation may be obtained by the profession of any faith, if only practice be directed by the rule of right and uprightness." It said that from this "noxious fountain" also issued the "absurd and noxious opinion that liberty of conscience should be assented to and maintained for every one." It also proclaimed the doctrine of Pope's Infallibility which was duly endorsed by the Council. Another Syllabus was issued by Pope Pius X in 1907 condemning the teachings of modernism under sixty-five headings.

Eastern Contribution

European struggle for religious freedom and rationalism was not purely a European enterprise. Even in their sorry plight, Hinduism and Buddhism made their own contribution to it. While Missionary-Imperialist Europe was contemptuous of the East, many thoughtful Europeans found in its religions a very different example and type — a type which is deep, relaxed, wise, and tolerant, a type which does not punish dissent, a type which does not worry whether you hold that the earth is flat or round, or whether it is five thousand or five-billion years old; in all these things it wants you to follow your best reason and stands for free inquiry. This exerted a silent but persistent influence on European intellect even when this influence remained unacknowledged.

Asia did not send out missionaries. But God made use of European scholars and missionaries to spread its message. They translated Eastern texts often to use them against their own religions. But things turned out differently. Many sensitive Europeans saw in them a deep intuition about spiritual things, an intuition they had not known before through their own religion. It is this influence that has been at the base of the New Age Movement. Eastern interiority, universalism and humanism rehabilitate reason as well as spirituality. Dogmatic and revelatory ideologies which are inimical to both feel subverted.

Conversion

In the spiritual world there are two important categories: God and your neighbour. You could look at your neighbour's God through his eyes, or could look at your neighbour through the eyes of your God. If you respect your neighbour and think that he is as good as you, then you will also think that his God is as good as your own. But if you think that he is no good,[11] then you also conclude that his God is no good and you would like to replace his God by your good God. This you do, not because you love your neighbour as you love yourself, but because if he is not a Christian, you are superior to him and need not love him. "Love thy neighbour" becomes "Watch thy neighbour, and convert him to the Sole Truth." Christian theology of conversion is based not only on an inadequate idea of God, but also on hatred of one's neighbour.

Be not afraid

Christian beliefs have neither rationality nor spirituality. But they are suited to certain minds and to a certain level of intellectual and moral development. There is now also a great vested interest in these beliefs. They are not going to be given up simply because they are foolish and morally and spiritually untenable.

"Be not afraid" to own them up, Pope John Paul says in a pep-talk using these Biblical words. He also uses these words as a rubric on the flap of his book making them almost the part of the title. If we remember the Biblical context, the words really mean: Do not be afraid of making claims for Jesus, for the Pope, for the Church. Be not afraid of claiming that the Christian God alone is true, that Jesus is his only and begotten Son, that salvation belongs to Christians alone, that the Church alone knows the

11. "You are not bad but cut out for better things and you could certainly become good by embracing the Christian God and its Saviour" — that is all the change the Second Vatican Council is contemplating.

truth and is the sole custodian of salvation. Be not afraid if the statements sound like nursery tales. Brazen it out. Say them and repeat them with a straight face and you will pass through. They may sound preposterous and arrogant to your own ears but your faith is on trial. Don't fail. Allow no intellectual or moral scruples to come in the way of your faith.

Index